QATARI SCHOOL LEADERSHIP
PORTRAITS:
LESSONS LEARNED FROM
EDUCATION FOR A NEW ERA REFORM

Hamad Bin Khalifa University Press
P O Box 5825
Doha, Qatar
www.hbkupress.com

Copyright © Dr. Asmaa Alfadala 2019
All rights reserved.

Cover photo: Turgaygundogdu's / Shutterstock.com

No part of this publication may be reproduced or transmitted in any form or by any means, electronic or mechanical, including photocopying, recording, or any information storage or retrieval system, without prior permission in writing from the publishers.
No responsibility for loss caused to any individual or organization acting on or refraining from action as a result of the material in this publication can be accepted by HBKU Press or the author.

ISBN: 9789927137778

Printed and bound in Doha Qatar.

Qatar National Library Cataloging-in-Publication (CIP)

Alfadala, Asmaa, author.

Qatari school leadership portraits : lessons learned from *Education for a New Era* reform / Dr. Asmaa Alfadala. - Doha : Hamad Bin Khalifa University Press, 2019.

pages ; cm

ISBN 978-992-713-777-8

1. School management and organization -- Qatar. 2. Educational leadership -- Qatar -- Case studies. 3. Educational change -- Qatar. I. Title.

LB2965.Q2 A65 2019
371.2095363 – dc 23   201927404043

QATARI SCHOOL LEADERSHIP PORTRAITS: LESSONS LEARNED FROM *EDUCATION FOR A NEW ERA* REFORM

CONTENTS

ACKNOWLEDGEMENTS 9

FOREWORD 11

EXECUTIVE SUMMARY 14

Chapter One:
THE CONTEXT 17
    The focus of the study: *Education for a New Era* 20
    Leadership Portraits: uniqueness of this book 22
    Structure of the book 25

Chapter Two:
QATARI EDUCATIONAL BACKGROUND 27
    Research context: *Education for a New Era* reform 27
        Qatar: a general overview 27
        Qatar's education system pre-reform 29
        Education for a New Era reform 30
        Challenges faced by school leaders in Qatar 34
    School leaders' perceptions of *Education for a New Era* 38
    Leaders' roles within change 40
    A model to explore leaders' perceptions in Qatar 42

Chapter Three:
PORTRAITURE AS A METHODOLOGY TO UNDERSTAND THE IMPLEMENTATION OF THE REFORM 47
    Portraiture in qualitative research 50
    Participants involved in the study 53
    My role 54

Chapter Four 57
FRUSTRATED LEADER IN A CHAOTIC CONTEXT 57
    Alnoor School 57
    Engines of the school: Amna and Mouna 58
    Parents' roles: problems in partnership 60

Workload and collaboration: implementation pressures vs.
pride in achievement 61
Multiplied workload 62
Factors contributing to increased workload 66
    Interruptions..66
    Lack of organization and planning: the reasons and
    consequences 68
Collaboration: management level vs. department level................70

Chapter Five:
A CARING LEADER MANAGING A CONSTANTLY FRANTIC TEAM 75
Doha School 75
Principal Salwa: leader as a mother figure................................. 79
Collaboration: good in parts...80
Leaders' responses to their challenging roles 82
Resistance to change 83
Dealing with the SEC's demands: a call for greater flexibility 85
Buying into the change 88
Substantial work(over)load 90
Emotional response to change 94

Chapter Six:
AN ISOLATED LEADER FACING VARIABLE STAFF COLLABORATION 97
Aljazeera School 97
Kawla and Lwloa: management styles 97
English and science departments: progressing well 101
Arabic and math departments: reform–led struggles
over collaboration and workforce shortage 106
Reasons behind workload 109
Variations in response to workload 111
Pressure from parents and the SEC... 113

Chapter Seven 117
EMPOWERING LEADER CONFRONTING DISRUPTIVE STUDENT BEHAVIOR.................................117
Gulf School 117
Student behavior: then and now... 119

Student misbehavior: the unpleasant consequences 122
Managing student behavior..124
Positive views about the reform...126
Implementation difficulties: ever–increasing paperwork 130
Artificial workloads...132
Training and professional development: growing difficulties 133
Resistance to change: a core leadership challenge 134
Challenges from the outside: ICT implementation 135
Decision-making and collaboration 137
Science department: struggle with collaboration........................ 140

Chapter Eight:
**GROUP PORTRAIT: CROSS–CASE ANALYSIS
AND DISCUSSION** **143**
   **Section 1: Leaders' perceptions of the reform and how
those leaders are managing the implementation** **145**
      Theme 1: Increasing responsibilities and workload................. 146
         Leaders' perceptions of workload 146
         Reasons behind workload 147
         Artificial workload..148
         Managing workload 150
      Theme 2: Collaboration 151
         The meaning of a collaborative school...............................152
         Positive examples 153
         Negative examples..155
         Leaders' roles in fostering collaboration 156
         Collaboration management 159
      Theme 3: The emotional responses to change...................... 161
         Identifying the emotional responses to change 162
         Types of emotions 163
            Positive emotions about the reform 163
            Negative emotions due to reform...................................164
         Managing emotions 166
      Theme 4: Conditions for change 168
         Leaders' perceptions of conditions for change................... 168
            Sufficient knowledge and skills 169
            Availability of resources 170
            Participation 171

  Commitment 173
  Leadership 174
 Constant change: a significant obstacle to change
 implementation 177

Section 2: Leaders' challenges in implementing the reform and how they responded to these issues 178
 Theme 5: Overall perceptions of challenges 179
  Internal challenges 180
   a) Interruptions 180
   b) Resistance to change 183
  External challenges 186
   a) Liaising with the SEC 186
   b) Communicating with parents 188

Chapter Nine:
LOOKING FORWARD: LESSONS LEARNED FROM THE QATARI EDUCATIONAL REFORM 193

REFERENCES 201

LIST OF TABLES
 Table 1. School numbers per year/cohort 47
 Table 2. Primary study participants 53
 Table 3. Positive and toxic schools 153
 Table 4. Leaders' challenges 180

LIST OF FIGURES
 Figure 1. Map of the State of Qatar 29
 Figure 2. Timeline of reform phases 34
 Figure 3. The National Professional Standards (NPS) 35
 Figure 4. Leaders are at the center of the "change tapestry" 44
 Figure 5. Group portrait glimpse 144
 Figure 6. The four main school leaders 145

ACKNOWLEDGEMENTS

Without the grace of Allah, I would never have accomplished this work. Writing a book was a lot harder than I imagined, but also vastly more rewarding. Of course, none of this would have been possible without my husband, Hamad, who stood by me during all of my struggles and successes. Thank you, Hamad, for believing in me and for your unwavering support, despite the social pressures you endured. I am also immensely grateful to my children (Latifa, Eisa, Shahd, Mohammed and Ali). Thank you, my dears, for your understanding and patience while I worked on this project. It is the joy and happiness that you give me every day that inspired me to complete this book.

I want to give a special thanks to my sister Ameena and my brother Mohammed for their ceaseless support and encouragement. Thank you, Ameena, for always being the person I could turn to during those dark and desperate years of study, research and writing; you sustained me in ways that I never knew I needed. A special expression of gratitude goes to my brother, Mohammed, who was always so confident that things would work out and never stopped motivating me to finish this work.

I'd also like to give special mention to my dissertation supervisor at Cambridge University, Dr. V. Darleen Opfer, for her invaluable advice, encouragement, and support. I was extremely lucky to have a supervisor who cared so much about my work, and who responded to my questions and queries so promptly. I would also like to acknowledge the very valuable input of Professor John Gray, for his patient guidance, encouragement, and advice during my time as a student.

I am also thankful to the many people who have contributed to this study, both directly and indirectly. Thanks to my friend Dr. Tasneem Amatullah, who edited several drafts of this work. Her comments and critical feedback were extremely helpful, and her encouragement even more so. My sincere thanks go to the four schools who participated in this study. Without their generosity in time and participation, this study would not have been possible.

Lastly, I am indebted to Qatar Foundation for Education, Science and Community Development and the World Innovation Summit for Education (WISE) for providing the funding for my research and supporting the publication of this book. I hope that through my work, I can pay it forward by making a positive contribution to the field.

FOREWORD

School leaders matter. Until recently, however, this understanding was limited in both research and practice. Lately, we've started to understand that while teachers account for more than a third of the variation in student success, school leaders contribute 25% to that variation (Louis et al., 2010). Thus, even though teachers have a direct influence over student learning, school leaders create the context and harness the multiple factors that are needed to improve schools at scale. And yet, we have very little understanding of how school leaders create these contexts and how they harness the factors that lead to success. We have even less knowledge of how they do that during significant reform efforts such as the *Education for a New Era* that Qatar began to undertake in 2004. *Qatari School Leadership Portraits: Lessons Learned from* Education for a New Era *Reform* provides a unique contribution to the field about the role of, and impacts on, school leaders as systems undergo a radical change. The research for this book was also conducted in a cultural context that has not often been a focus of education research, thus providing another valuable contribution.

I was not at RAND when the *Education for a New Era* reform was designed. I came to RAND just as the data for this book was being collected. From my colleagues, I learned that, of all the educational improvement options presented to the Qatari government, the most complex was selected, and an ambitious timeline for implementation was determined. The planned changes would require a radical transformation of every aspect of the system: from structure and governance to assessment and accountability; and from educator preparation and professional development to curriculum and pedagogical practices. By the time I started working on the continued implementation of the reforms, it had become clear that too much change had been implemented too quickly for the system and its personnel to adapt and that the developmental needs of educators had been greatly underestimated. This book, *Qatari School Leadership Portraits*, illustrates these problems and the ways that school leaders in the system were impacted by them. Importantly, the book also portrays the ways that the school leaders managed to lead within this context. It shows how, even within a constantly changing system, school leaders can support change processes.

Dr. Alfadala shows these portraits of change leadership by utilizing a unique framework she has named a change tapestry. The change tapestry considers both the aspects of the context for which management is needed, including an understanding of the changes necessary, managing the changes, and sustaining the changes and the change tools that can be drawn upon by school leaders to put the changes in motion and maintain them over time. Considering the intersection of the conditions which need to be managed and the tools that school leaders could use provides a unique lens to understand the school leaders' actions in Qatar. *Education for a New Era* created a problematic context for change which school leaders needed an understanding of to deploy the right change tools that could help their teachers to implement the reform. The portraits of school leaders presented in this book help us to understand how they made sense of the changes that were necessary to achieve *Education for a New Era* and how that understanding resulted in the choices they made to deploy change tools they had at their disposal.

The field of education has concluded that school leaders successfully manage change when they: recruit and motivate high-quality teachers; identify and articulate school vision and goals; effectively allocate resources; and develop organizational structures to support instruction and learning (Horng, Kalogrides, & Loeb, 2010). But this understanding of what is necessary for successful change management does not consider how the change (and changing) context might both limit and afford school leaders' abilities to implement the requisite actions for successful implementation. The *Education for a New Era* reforms raise questions

about how Qatari school leaders could successfully manage change given how these reforms were administered at the national level:
- How do you motivate and recruit quality teachers for a change that is radically different from the education system in which they've previously worked?
- How do you articulate a vision and set goals for reform that you do not entirely understand?
- How do you effectively allocate resources when you've never been in control of resources before? And,
- How do you develop organizational structures to support instruction and learning when you are trying to support the implementation of pedagogical practices you have little previous experience with?

The portraits of school leaders in Qatar, described in this book, help to provide answers to these questions, an understanding of how educators make sense of unclear and complicated reforms, and how they act to be as effective as possible within this context. The book also provides valuable lessons about the ways that future reform efforts, in Qatar and other countries, should be managed for change to occur.

V. Darleen Opfer, PhD

Vice President and Director, RAND Education and Labor

Distinguished Chair in Education Policy

EXECUTIVE SUMMARY

Qatar was and is keen to improve the education system as a whole and for Qatari students to thrive and prosper in a more diversified economy. In 2004, Qatar adopted *Education for a New Era* reform that focused on school autonomy by decentralizing from the former Ministry of Education, introducing innovative curricula, building variety in academic focus and presenting more choice for parents in determining where to send their children based on their interests. The ENE reform steered in a vigorous state committed to improve Qatar's education system. Nevertheless, the ENE reform was extremely complex, and its implementation had created multiple challenges for school leaders.

While discussions on educational leadership and policies are not new, there is little research that explores Qatari school leaders' experiences amidst an educational reform. *Qatari School Leadership Portraits* fills that gap. We often approach policy issues from a political standpoint failing to understand the 'greater good' in it. However, my research has convinced me that an education system must have a human focus: a focus on the individual student's talents and capacities, and on teachers and leaders, the core stakeholders of teaching and learning. Therefore, in this book, I narrate the perspectives of school leaders from four schools who experienced the ENE reform; lived within it; maneuvered it to their best; and learned from it despite facing challenges.

Leaders are key to carrying out the changes mandated by the reform. Keeping leaders' perceptions and experiences at the core of this analysis, I draw from different change models in the literature and develop a model to explore Qatari leaders' perceptions as detailed in the second chapter. Further, by using a qualitative approach, I impart to the reader a more acute understanding of the decisions made throughout the reform from the insightful perspectives of individual school leaders and their teams, including heads of department and teachers.

Four school portraits presented in this book illustrate how different school leaders navigated the new changes due to the implementation of ENE reform. While Alnoor School had Amna and Mouna as engines of the school leading in a chaotic school context, Doha School had Salwa, a caring leader who was managing a constantly frantic team through collaboration. Aljazeera School had dedicated leaders Kawla and Lwloa; the management styles varied and so did the staff collaboration. Some departments in Aljazeera School were under the reform-led struggles due to workforce shortage while some departments were progressing well. Saeed, the leader of Gulf School, had issues due to disruptive student behavior, yet he excelled as an empowering leader. Finally, the group portrait or the cross-case analysis examines these four school portraits together, unpacking the similarities and differences under five main themes: workload, collaboration, emotional response to change, conditions for change, and leaders' challenges.

Ultimately, *Qatari School Leadership Portraits* speaks to the past and the present of Qatar's education system. It reflects on the importance of school leaders' role amidst the reform, and the progress that has been made by the implementation of the reform despite several challenges that school leaders and teachers have encountered. This book is to champion the main agents of change, the school leaders, and to present a case for additional policies that provide professional development for both school leaders and teachers in Qatar's schools of today and tomorrow.

Chapter One

THE CONTEXT

The education system in Qatar has recently experienced a major shift in organizational leadership. After twelve years of implementing the *Education for a New Era* (ENE) reform under the Supreme Education Council (SEC), the state has returned to a system led by the Ministry of Education (MoE). Public education is essential for a country to maintain competitiveness in today's globalized economy. Over the past 50 years, Qatar's publicly funded education system and institutions have undergone radical changes. One dramatic change was the adoption of the *Education for a New Era* reform which occurred in 2004 along with the introduction of independent schools. This new school model focused on school autonomy and decoupled individual schools from a central state Ministry of Education authority. The autonomy of schools encourages teachers and leaders to be innovative in developing curricula and creative in delivering content instruction. The expectation was that this curricular independence would increase administrative accountability because the new system builds variety in academic focus, allowing parents to have more choice in determining where to send their children based on their interests. As all eyes were on Qatar, the education reform was perceived as a test case for radical education overhauls in the Middle East (Coker, 2010).

I am one of the Qatari educators who was encouraged by the shakeup of the system and the new objectives set by the ENE. I worked as a physics teacher for six years in Qatar's Ministry of Education schools and as Head of the Science Department in a primary school after the reform. Both in my personal and professional orientations, I was often preoccupied with my classroom practices and leadership style, as well as my own professional development needs. I am an educator who believes that the reforms work to improve the education system as a whole and for Qatari students, making them more creative and critical thinkers enabling them to be leaders in the competitive global market. This position is not without its detractors, or else we would not have reverted back to the original system; some policymakers, educators and community members formed a negative opinion of the reforms, and that opposition may have hampered the full implementation of the reforms as they were originally designed. In addition to my professional experience in the Qatari school system, I have also worked for the RAND Corporation as a policy analyst, the corporation that suggested the implementation of the ENE reform. In this capacity, I was able to observe the policy development and implementation of the public education system reforms related to *Education for a New Era* from outside of the system that I know so well from teaching within it.

The Qatari education system is centered on how to best prepare students to thrive and prosper in a more diversified economy that needs and encourages entrepreneurship and creative problem-solving. Such characteristics can be developed when the skills needed are taught to future Qatari leaders of business, education, technology, and so forth—that is, to students. We often approach policy issues from a political position: one based on a logic of providing a program that may not be ideal for all citizens, but is perceived as being provided for the 'greater good.' However, my research has convinced me that an education system has to have a human focus: a focus on the individual student's talents and capacities, and on teachers and leaders, the core stakeholders of teaching and learning. Therefore, I present in this book the perspective of school leaders from four schools who experienced the ENE reform; lived within it; manuevered it to their best; and learned from it despite facing challenges.

The ENE reform, along with the creation of independent schools, ushered in a new approach that emphasized independence and allowed school leadership to cultivate a school identity. Along with the new system came a new governing body, the Supreme Education Council (SEC). Until this point, the K-12 education system had been regulated by the Ministry of Education (MoE), a highly centralized office that "oversaw all aspects of public education and many aspects of private education" (Brewer et al., 2007, p. 21). The national curriculum under the MoE tended to rely on traditional methods of learning such as rote memorization which does not stimulate students nor allow for student-teacher interaction, in contrast to ENE which encourages creativity and development of critical thinking skills.

The SEC was designed to modernize and professionalize the lackluster system under the MoE. Other notable deficiencies of the former system included an absence of performance indicators for both student progress and school capacity. Within an educational system where the authority was centralized in the government, teachers and administrators were provided with little to no actionable performance information—not that it would have made much of a difference in school performance, because school officials were not granted the authority to make changes. To add to the challenges faced by the education system under the MoE, the national investment in education was relatively small. This was reflected in the low teacher salaries and resources for professional development. It was not only the human resources that were neglected, but also the education infrastructure, which was in poor condition. Many school buildings were in disrepair and classrooms were overcrowded (Brewer et al., 2007).

Qatari leadership began to realize that their education system was insufficient and unable to turn out graduates with the skills necessary to participate in the increasingly competitive global economy. For instance, Qatar's economy is currently dominated by oil and natural gas extractive sectors. The workforce necessary for this industry has to develop highly technical skills, and in many cases, must be educated to the graduate level in order to be able to contribute to the expansion of the national economy. Furthermore, a majority portion of the Qatari technical workforce consists of expat workers from countries with more advanced education systems. The ENE reform ushered in a vigorous state commitment to education. Under the former MoE system, Qatar was known to have the least capital investment in education among the Gulf Cooperation Council (GCC) countries. Subsequent to the implementation of ENE reforms, Qatar not only led all countries in the GCC on educational spending but also rose to the 36th rank in the world. To put this rapid progression in educational spending in a regional context, the UAE ranked 41st, Bahrain 48th, Kuwait 54th, the KSA 57th, and Oman 84th in the world. This increase in capital expenditure clearly indicates a shift in the way the state values its education system.

The issue of education reform is very important to me as a professional Qatari woman who has experience with the former education system and profound access to developments of the new ENE policy. I had a deep sense of national and local engagement and the urgent need to explore the educational reform and its development throughout the country. Between my years as an educator and then as an analyst, I gained a precise perspective concerning the education reform and the success it engendered. I will share my experience and insights with you throughout this book.

The focus of the study: *Education for a New Era*

In this book, I introduce you to school leaders from four Qatari schools that are working within the context of the educational reform, *Education for a New Era*. I use the term 'leaders' for persons who are leading or implementing the changes outlined in the ENE policy. These education leaders work in what we have termed independent schools. These are publicly funded, privately run schools (similar to charter schools in other countries) established through the education reform in Qatar. These four institutions were part of Generation I (cohort one) schools which were opened in fall 2004 (Brewer et al., 2007, p. xxxv).

The ENE reform introduced changes into the country's education system. Under the original MoE system, our schools lacked a standards-based curriculum as well as professional development programs for teachers and leaders. In addition to providing these staples of a modernized, progressive education system, the ENE also provided a new system for assessing student progress. These positive reforms began to make improvements to the Qatar school system; however, as summed up in a 2007 RAND Corporation report, "despite the many positive effects of the reform, more change is needed to support schools and teachers" (Zellman et al., 2009).

The ENE reform is extremely complex, and its implementation has created multiple challenges for school leaders. The focus of this book is to narrate how school leaders navigate this context of widespread change. Post-reform, the new school model in Qatar has increased both autonomy and accountability for these leaders (Brewer et al., 2007). In accordance with the new focus on autonomy and accountability, I approach leadership as a social practice, rather than a list of skills. For example, school principals have a central role in the implementation of educational change, and many researchers focus on the role of principals in reform (Leithwood & Jantzi, 1990; McLaughlin & Mitra, 2001). My book stands out due to its qualitative approach to understand the in-depth narratives of these principals' experiences with reform (Fullan, 2001b; Johnson, 1998; Orr, Byrne-Jiminez, McFarlane & Brown, 2005). I contend that we need to understand the role of school principals within the context of school reform in Qatar from their own perspectives. We must understand the role of school leaders in order to facilitate an understanding of the development of the ENE system, and more broadly, Qatar's global ranking in the world of leadership and education.

Throughout this book, I impart to the reader a more acute understanding of the decisions made throughout the reform from the insightful perspectives of individual school leaders. I develop an effective representation and critique of the notion of 'leadership' within the evolving school system. To do this, I draw on reflections of my own professional approach to educational leadership based on my own experience as an insider within Qatari schools, both pre- and post-reform. Along with my own professional experience, I combine observations of the transition process and interview data from a group of school leaders to inform my analysis and draw conclusions. Through this process, I demonstrate how my knowledge about the education of school leaders themselves, in terms of their professional development, have evolved in order to present a holistic understanding of leadership experience. Furthermore, while collecting data for this book, I was able to witness many great practices in the schools that I observed. I met school leaders who have learned from mistakes made in implementing the (ENE) reforms and who now see students embracing the individualized pursuit of education. I communicate my findings and explain why I came to the conclusion that school leaders need much greater support to implement the reform process. I would like to acknowledge up front that this book is neither written from a policy perspective nor solely targeting the academicians. This book is instead the lived experiences, the narratives, the portraits of four Qatari school leaders experiencing and navigating the reform. Unlike other books or policy papers, I do not provide readers with ready-made answers or quick-fix solutions; rather, I invite you to be reflective and critique these leadership experiences and my reflections as I engage in this study keeping the context in mind. This book is an explorative journey calling for educational leaders to create collaborative cultures in their schools. To this end, I take you through my study of leadership practices within the wider context of education reform. Consequently, your personal and professional appreciation of school leadership will grow, especially in relation to the quest for excellence in the overall reform of schools.

Leadership Portraits: uniqueness of this book

Qatar's endeavour for education reform has been going on for 15 years. The fieldwork for this study was carried out during part of the eighth year of the reform, from September 2011 to January

2012. Under the ENE reform, the actual job descriptions of Qatari school leaders has evolved considerably. The new description relates to the National Professional Standards (NPS) for leaders, which are discussed in Chapter Two. In what follows, I consider the perceptions of leaders in relation to their new job descriptions in six of the following crucial areas:

1. Leading and managing change
2. Leading and developing people and teams
3. Developing and managing school-community relations
4. Developing and managing resources
5. Reflecting on, evaluating and improving leadership and management
6. Developing, communicating and reporting on the strategic vision and aims of the school community

This book is unique because it presents a personal look at the reform through the perceptions of school leaders and their teams, including heads of department and teachers. I use National Professional Standards as a measurement tool to explore the six crucial areas of analysis, as it will be relevant to the four schools where I undertook this study. It offers a broader understanding of the extant perceptions supportive of successful school leadership. The book demonstrates the importance of educational institutions in general, and schools in particular, to understand the delivery of the ENE reform. My hope is that this book will help guide appropriate support from policymakers being provided to assist school leaders in the implementation of such innovation more rapidly and more effectively.

The primary reason for focusing on leaders' perceptions is that, in my view, leaders are at the heart of any educational change (Fullan, 1991; Fullan & Hargreaves, 1991). I argue that leaders need to understand their new roles and the challenges they face within the specific context of the reform and its implementation. This book will also aid decision-makers in understanding the perceptions of school leadership and the skills required for such leadership. Consequently, this nuanced understanding may contribute to a reframing of the reform, which could have the benefit of procuring greater support for its future implementation.

Keeping leaders' perceptions and experiences at the core of this analysis, I take a thematic approach using change models for the theoretical framework. This approach recognizes the importance of considering a subject's perceptions within the process of implementing policy change. Leaders are key to carrying out the changes mandated by the reform; therefore, identifying their concerns in relation to innovation is essential in facilitating the reform's requirements (Hord, Rutherford, Huling-Austin, & Hall, 1987). Drawing from different change models in the literature, I developed a model to explore Qatari leaders' perceptions as detailed in Chapter 2, Figure 4.

I reviewed the data produced over the past three decades concerning Qatari education, and I found a gap. There has been very little critical discussion of the perceptions of school leaders regarding the reform. School leaders' perceptions constitute a relatively unexplored research area—a knowledge gap. *Qatari School Leadership Portraits* fills that gap. The reform's introduction encourages researchers to provide information that will contribute to an enhanced understanding of the large-scale change involved. School leaders play a role that makes a critical difference in implementing the reform, and it is vital that their perceptions are discussed within the larger debate about education reform in Qatar.

Throughout this book, we will explore the perceptions and practices of school leaders within the context of the reform, as well as any role identifications that may be related to those perceptions. This book is to champion the main agents of change, the school leaders, and to present a case for additional policies that provide professional development for both school leaders and teachers in Qatar's schools of today and tomorrow.

The narrative of this book revolves around the following questions:

1. How do school leaders interpret school change and its place in *Education for a New Era*?
2. How do school leaders manage the reform, particularly within the context of their changing job description?
3. What challenges do school leaders face, at both the organizational and the individual level when implementing the *Education for a New Era* reform, and its requirements?
4. How do school leaders respond to the challenges they encounter in implementing this change in schools?

This study adopts a qualitative approach, using interviews, observation and document analysis derived within four primary schools in Qatar. Drawing on the work of Sara Lawrence-Lightfoot (1983), I created a portrait of each school to develop a fuller picture of the issues and complexities facing school leaders experiencing change. Five main themes emerged from the data analysis: workload, collaboration, conditions for change, emotional response to that change, and challenges for leaders. These are discussed in the later chapters.

Structure of the book

Qatari School Leadership Portraits consists of nine chapters that begin by setting the wider context of the research within which this study's purpose and significance are framed. Following that, in Chapter Two, I share relevant literature about educational models of change and leadership within the context of Qatari education. Chapter Three describes the methodology employed in data collection and analysis, in addition to a discussion of my epistemological stance as a researcher. Chapters Four through Seven are comprised of the evidence from fieldwork with an emphasis on four case studies presented as portraits of each school. Next, in Chapter Eight, a "group portrait" presents the cross-case analysis and a critical discussion of the findings. The narrative concludes in Chapter Nine, which will summarize the study findings, also discussing lessons learned from the educational reform in Qatar.

Chapter Two

QATARI EDUCATIONAL BACKGROUND

Leadership is the key to dealing with obstacles within the change process. In this chapter you will read about the ENE reform, with a focus on school leadership challenges, within the Qatari context. Research on educational and organizational change has found the process of such change to be characterized by a variety of predictable obstacles, including shifting and unclear goals, lack of communication of the school vision, lack of understanding and interest, lack of resources, staff resistance, and absence of leadership for the change (Drucker, 1995; Evans, 1996; Fullan, 2001a; Hall and Hord, 2006; Kotter, 2002). Therefore, it is necessary to further explore other processes linked to change, as well as how these processes affect reform in educational institutions.

Research context: *Education for a New Era* reform

Qatar: a general overview

Qatar has implemented a multitude of sweeping social and economic reforms to spur future growth and development (Planning Council, 2007). The focus of these reforms was the development of a sustainable future Qatari workforce. Currently, the workforce in Qatar mainly consists of a large expatriate community. However, Qatar is a state with a clear and unambiguous national mission statement focused on developing a Qatari-centered workforce. Educational rationales and objectives are being developed around human talent in an attempt to decrease the country's dependency on the expatriate communities, assist in international competitiveness, and inspire highly educated Qataris for the overall benefit of the nation.

A good example of this effort can be found at Education City, which consists entirely of international university campuses

(Knight, 2014). The reform initiative in education, then, is clearly critical to the success of the larger reform effort. Qatar's main wealth and income may be derived from natural resources such as oil (Qatar Knowledge Economy Project, 2007), but the research questions of this study are embedded in the context of another kind of wealth: the educational change currently occurring in Qatar.

A description of the State of Qatar and its political system informs the parameters of the discussion of education policy processes. Qatar is an Arab and Islamic state geographically located on a much smaller peninsula on the northeast coast of the larger Arabian Peninsula. Qatar happens to be one of the smallest nations in the Gulf region, with a total land area of 11,437 square km, and a total population of 2.83 million (Qatar Statistics Authority, 2019). The official language of the state is Arabic, although English has emerged as a medium of communication in the private business sector (Gonzalez, Karoly, Constant, Salem & Goldman, 2008).

Qatar's economy has evolved over time. At the beginning of the twentieth century, Qatar's economy was based on camel breeding, pearl diving, and fishing (Gonzalez et al., 2008). Since the 1960s, Qatar's economy has been almost exclusively funded by substantial oil reserves and major natural gas deposits (Qatar Knowledge Economy Project, 2007). Under new leadership in 1995, Qatar's economy began to excel, which drove a modernization program led by the father of the current Amir of Qatar, His Highness Sheikh Hamad bin Khalifa Al Thani. He introduced socio-political liberalization, including comprehensive, large-scale education reform, women's enfranchisement, and a new and more liberal constitution. Other developments he can take credit for include the creation of Al Jazeera, a leading global English and Arabic news broadcast and media company. Additionally, his vision of Qatar as a global player included the founding of a knowledge-based economy facilitated by extensive educational reform (Qatar Knowledge Economy Project, 2007).

Figure 1. Map of the State of Qatar

Qatar's education system pre-reform

Before the reform, educational practices in Qatar were similar to those in the majority of other Gulf and non-Gulf Arab systems. In those systems, emphasis has always been placed upon 'learning by rote' memorization, with little attention given to critical thinking or the development of problem-solving skills. The original system insisted on the primacy of learning the Arabic language so students could effectively study the Quran in both verbal and written forms. Young males were taught in the *kuttab*, a school located in a mosque. The same system applied to young females, but they were taught within the home. Learned men or women would come and teach girls inside their houses, with family supervision (US Library of Congress, 1994). Eventually, a total of 12 *katatib* (plural for place of learning) would be created, which both boys and girls attended. With time, other subjects such as geography, English, arithmetic, and Islamic studies were introduced to expand the curriculum studied by both boys and girls; however, the system maintained a focus on memory-based learning. This effectively rewarded the correct regurgitation of information as taught and seen, with little emphasis placed upon a more critical evaluation, the production of ideas, or the encouragement of more independent thoughts.

The Ministry of Education (*Wizarat Al Maarif*) took over for two decades in the 1950s and 1960s. During that period, the ministry essentially copied the Egyptian system of education, importing both books and teachers from Egypt and other Arab countries to educate the Qatari population. In an attempt to localize the education process, Qatar began printing its own textbooks in 1965. With the adoption of the Egyptian system came a broader curriculum where additional disciplines and subjects were being covered; yet effective communication and critical thinking were not prioritized. In the absence of key components of creative and independent thinking, such as problem-solving skills, any notion of further innovation within the educational system was stifled, and the need for some kind of reform grew obvious. In fact, the Egyptian system lasted until the modern reforms were introduced into the Qatari educational system at the beginning of this century. Despite its longevity, the Egyptian system was perceived as lacking in many key areas in comparison with Western education models. This growing perception, coupled with an increased drive to embrace modern international business practices, became the catalyst for Qatari leaders to concede that the old system was failing to deliver. To this end, His Highness Sheikh Hamad bin Khalifa Al Thani commissioned the RAND Corporation to do a national assessment of the educational system in Qatar, taking the first major step towards true education reform.

Education for a New Era reform

It was 2001 when the government contracted the RAND Corporation to examine the public education system provided by the

MoE. At the time of the RAND study, there was a consensus among Qatar's leaders that the existing MoE system of public education was not producing high-quality educational, social, and economic outcomes for Qatari learners, or for society as a whole; further, the system appeared to be out of alignment with the educational needs of a wealthy country seeking 21st-century global competitiveness (Brewer et al., 2007). The RAND study was carried out between September 2001 and May 2002. A team of nine interdisciplinary researchers began on-site investigations in October 2001. The team had three goals:

1. to describe and understand the Qatari school system,
2. to identify problems with that system, and
3. to recommend approaches for improving the performance of schools and students within the system (Brewer et al., 2007, p. 33).

The project was a priority for the state, which offered the RAND team access to a coordinating committee that included high-ranking decision-makers, both Qatari and non-Qatari. This coordinating committee was tasked with helping the research team discover and understand the social and cultural context. RAND conducted observations at 15 schools, analyzing the primary, preparatory and secondary levels. The team gathered additional information through focus groups with teachers, students and parents. The thorough data collection process included approximately 200 interviews with key people responsible for the provision of education, namely school personnel, students, parents, and representatives from the MoE as well as other ministers. RAND also gathered data from documents, including student test scores, curriculum materials and regulations.

The MoE system was found to perpetuate a number of issues that were holding back educational progress. Specifically, observers identified a lack of vision for setting of adequate educational goals, piecemeal growth without an overall consideration of the whole system, an inflexible hierarchical organizational structure, unclear lines of authority, top-down control of curriculum and teaching, and a lack of training and professional development (see Brewer et al., 2007). Despite the weaknesses in the Qatari education system, the RAND team did identify some positive areas, including familiarity with international development, enthusiastic and committed staff, desire for autonomy and change, and the acceptance of alternative schooling options (Brewer et al., 2007).

The wholesale reform of the education system began with the replacement of the Ministry of Education with a new institution to direct the national public education policy. The Supreme Education Council (SEC) was established by Amiri Decree No. 37 in November 2002. The SEC is a semi-governmental agency charged with overseeing and implementing education reform, including the work of its operational institutes, which are responsible for the practical success of *Education for a New Era*. The education reform called for the development of a completely new education system independent of the MoE, which was phased out in October 2009 and replaced with the SEC.

Based on RAND's analysis, the research team worked with national leaders to develop a plan "informed by evidence on education reform around the world, yet situated to the Qatari situation" (Brewer et al., 2007, p. 9). The RAND Corporation recommended several options for the new system: a modified centralized model, a charter school model, and a voucher model. The option selected by the Qatari government was the independent (charter) schools model. RAND went on to further refine this model, and to tailor it to a Qatari context suggesting the implementation of new charter schools in Qatar called the Independent Schools (Brewer et al., 2007).

The newly implemented Independent Schools Model represented a move to a more decentralized system of schooling than had previously existed in Qatar. The system created latitude for many more schooling options. It dramatically reduced the level of centralized control and created more room for monitoring and evaluation of students, administrators, and schools in the context of a system of accountability with increased parental choice.

The initial goal was achieved. The Qatari education system was diversified by generating a variety of schooling alternatives with different missions, curricula, pedagogy, and resource allocation models. To accompany increased independence, school leadership would be held accountable for the quality of education through increased transparency about school progress, parental choice, and minimal government oversight (Brewer et al., 2007, p. 58).

The new Qatari system included international benchmarked curriculum standards, national testing based on those standards, independent government-funded schools, and parental choice informed by annual school report cards. This reform was designed to improve global competitiveness via the educational system. As (Davies, 2005) states, educational reform worldwide has embraced standardization as the solution to raising standards and improving economic competitiveness. The ENE met the objective "to create an educational system based on an internationally benchmarked curriculum, global best practice and Islamic values in a technologically emerging society. ENE did not just adopt modern technology; it attempted to provide leaders in future technology and research" (Anderson, Alnaimi & Alhajri, 2010).

The *Education for a New Era* reform has been implemented gradually, in three distinct but overlapping phases (see Figure 2). During Phase I, ministry-operated schools were unaffected because the RAND plan called for a system that would work in parallel with the old system (MoE) in order to minimize disruption. The first independent schools, referred to as the Generation I schools, opened in 2004. According to Brewer et al. (2007, p. xxxv), an independent school is "a publicly funded, privately run school (similar to a charter school in other countries) established through the education reform in Qatar." The Education and Evaluation institutes were also established during Phase I, to build the organizational and policy infrastructure required for the first cohort, Generation I schools.

Phase II began with the opening of the first cohort of schools. This phase was instrumental for data gathering and decision-making. During this phase, the RAND team collected data essential to inform the Qatari leadership's decision-making process as to whether or not moving to an independent school model would be optimal.

Phase III is focused on the Qatari leadership's decision regarding the continuation of the new model. The committee decided to proceed with the reform plan and all the MoE schools were phased out in 2009. According to the SEC, the current school system for the academic year 2013–14 served 98,332 students enrolled in independent schools comprising 47 kindergartens, 101 primary schools, 56 preparatory schools and 53 secondary schools.

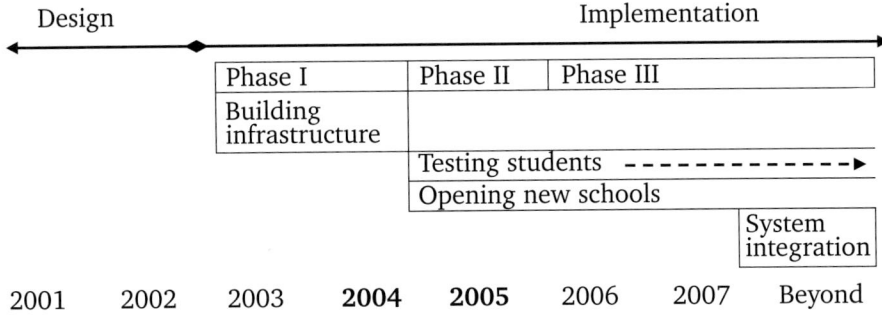

Figure 2. Timeline of reform phases (Brewer et al., 2007, p. 81)

Challenges faced by school leaders in Qatar

As you may imagine, the complex nature of the reform—a near total replacement of the former system with a new model—has affected practices in school leadership. One major contribution of the reform is the introduction of National Professional Standards (NPS). Introducing these standards had a significant impact on leaders' roles, resulting in several distinct system innovations. As in Figure 3, the NPS are a set of key requirements introduced to enable school leaders to implement the changes effectively. The requirements are:

1. Leading and managing change
2. Leading and developing people and teams

3. Developing and managing school-community relations
4. Developing and managing resources
5. Reflecting on, evaluating and improving leadership and management
6. Developing, communicating and reporting on the strategic vision and aims of the school community

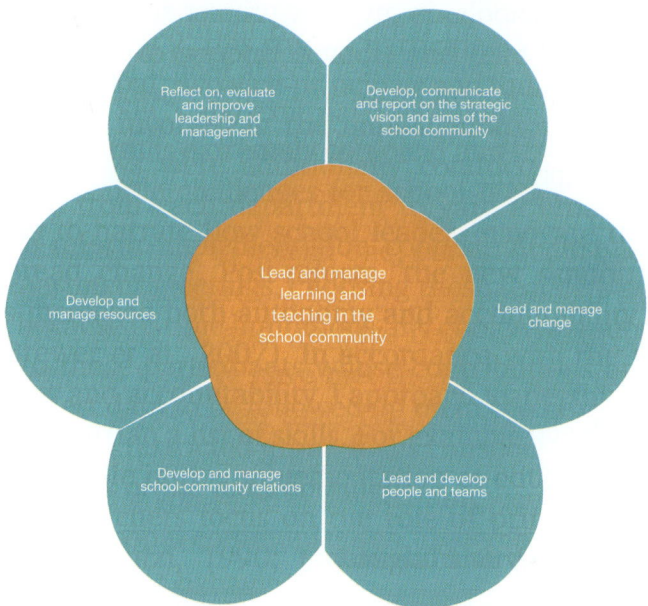

Figure 3. The National Professional Standards (NPS) (SEC, 2009, p. 6)

The NPS were implemented in 2004, and despite the progress made, leaders continue to face challenges brought on by the reform's consistently evolving nature and the resulting dramatic changes. The focus of the analysis will be upon school leaders from cohorts one and two.

An early review study by RAND was conducted over a two-year period from 2005–07. It evaluated the progress of the reform within 16 schools and found that the schools were still facing many challenges, including curriculum development, classroom pedagogy, professional development, lack of parental involvement, and student achievement (Constant et al., 2010, p. 459). The study revealed that school leaders believed that the constantly changing policies imposed by the SEC had negatively affected their work and contributed to a misunderstanding of the reform concept as a whole. This perception appears to have become a long-standing one and it was reiterated by the Evaluation Institute's former Director Adel Alsayed in a 2008 interview, where he noted, "frequent changes in policies damage the educational system and affect the results of independent schools. In my view greater stability is called for." This is a point of view shared by Zellman and colleagues (2009), who also advocate a limit on policy change. Clearly, schools require more stability through structured long- and short-term planning to minimize disruptions.

Implementation is not the end of the story: change involves more than simply putting the reform into practice, a process more complicated than might appear on the surface. Change necessarily begets complexity and, as Everard et al. (2004) state, implementation entails "a process of interaction, dialogue, feedback, modifying objectives, recycling plans, coping with mixed feelings and values, pragmatism, micropolitics, frustration, patience and muddle" (2004, p. 240).

Thus, implementing change does not involve a fixed 'blueprint'; rather, it is an interaction between members of the organization and the context, achieved through dialogue, suggested by modifications, and achieved via feedback. Leaders need to adapt to and deal with these constantly, as unanticipated issues are triggered during the change process. Given the context of the Qatari educational reform and the challenges faced by leaders, it is necessary to consider some central aspects of leadership: leadership definitions, leaders' perceptions and roles, and the characteristics of effective leadership.

To evaluate the progress of the reform, RAND conducted case studies of 12 independent schools and four ministry schools. Data was collected over a period of two years from 2005 to 2007 (see: Constant et al., 2010; Zellman, Constant & Goldman, 2011). This RAND study reveals both positive indicators of improvement and tremendous challenges to implementation. The study claims that students in independent schools are now in more learner-centered classrooms with improved facilities, where better prepared and better trained teachers guide them in accordance with internationally benchmarked standards (Zellman et al., 2011, p. 4). Although some progress has been made, substantial challenges remain, including curriculum development, classroom pedagogy, professional development, parental involvement and student achievement, as well as school autonomy and accountability (Zellman et al., 2011). While the purpose of this book is not to discuss these challenges in detail, I must point out the importance of addressing these difficulties as a means of presenting the complexity of the issues school leaders face.

The educational reform in Qatar was initiated in the early 2000s. This study explores the features of the reform during its implementation phase. I must point out what Fullan (1991) articulates well. In this analysis we experience successes and setbacks because change is not a linear process, and phases of change can overlap. Fullan (1991) points out stages of change process: mobilization, implementation and institutionalization. Leaders in the change process, including the transition between each stage, can expect both progression and regression. The actual experience of the implementation of the ENE supports the accuracy of this position. Further, Fullan and Stigelbauer (1991) identify three factors, namely characteristics of change, local characteristics and external factors: government and local agencies. In the Qatari case these three categories undoubtedly play a major role in determining how the reform takes place. The book specifically focuses on the critical role of school leaders in carrying out the ENE reform, and on how these three characteristics shape their experience.

Due consideration must therefore be given to the current nature and stage of the Qatari reform, specifically whether it exhibits the features of the implementation phase indicated by Fullan (1991) and Kotter (1996), or has evolved into a more mature and embedded reform; also, which factors are affecting its progress. These questions will be explored in further detail in Chapter Eight, Group Portrait: Cross-Case Analysis and Discussion.

School leaders' perceptions of *Education for a New Era*

My experience and observations as an educator lead me to emphasize that, in fact, a key component to the conceptualization of effective leadership is that it is an interactive process between leadership, staff and the institutional context. We have to consider that educating people, agenda-setting and redesigning organizations are all complex processes which involve substantial staff interactions. Given the empirical evidence that I have collected, I propose a more inclusive definition of leadership: one which reflects a more interactive and dynamic process.

We will apply this conceptualization to the analysis of testimonies of leaders as they implement educational reform. Additionally, I identify the choices and actions available to leaders as they manage the complexity of this process of change. In doing so, I highlight the research context and the challenges facing school leadership; then I focus on the "practices" of leadership and the role principals play in affecting the implementation of the reform.

School leaders' perceptions regarding educational reform tell us a lot about the progress of the reforms and the direction in which they are going. However, perceptions are not observable, so my approach is to observe school leaders' practices and question them about their motivations and experiences as a means to understanding their roles within that change. Questioning leaders about the choices they make offers insight into their perceptions. Understanding perceptions provides key insights into the processes that drive decision-making and influence the behavior of leaders in managing educational change. Additionally, a person's perception correlates to his or her opinion, understanding, belief and insight, all of which are invisible. Therefore, in order to explore school leaders' perceptions, I observed their visible practices and actual behavior in leading change.

Under the ENE, Qatar has undergone a fundamental educational change since 2004. This includes changes in school structure, assessment mechanisms, and a new curriculum. The reform has been a colossal endeavour in both scope and depth; because of this, all education sector stakeholders have been involved in coping with the reform. School leaders are crucial to this process of change, and given the position and responsibilities they hold in change management, it is unrealistic to merely assume that the individuals involved in implementing the change will necessarily understand, or completely believe in, that change (Leonard, 1996). Different perspectives on the reform will yield different responses to the change process. Since school leaders are at the center of the change process, their perceptions are one of the key variables within change management and leadership (Fullan, 1991). For this reason, school leaders' perceptions warrant an in-depth study. Understanding how school leaders interpret the reform may provide a more comprehensive picture of the change process.

Leader perceptions are influenced by their individually held values and beliefs, which suggests that leaders' interpretations will be translated into practices based on these values and beliefs. For Sergiovanni (1992),

> The heart of leadership has to do with what a person believes, values, dreams about and is committed to, but it is more than vision. It is the person's interior world, reflection combined with personal vision and an internal system of values, which becomes the basis of leadership strategies and actions. (p. 7)

Sergiovanni (1992) states that a school leader should be "doing the things right" and that each has to decide whether they are "doing the right things right" (p. 7). He argues that values and commitment provide the kind of inspiration, meaning, and motivation that "come from within" and that the school is a community comprised of relationships and diverse values, commitments, and obligations. Leadership decisions and actions are a reflection of school leaders' interior worlds. In order to explore their perceptions, it is important to consider what they value and believe. Their choices and decision-making for leading change are closely connected with these values and beliefs.

Leaders' roles within change

The complexity of school leaders' roles has been discussed widely in the literature. Shields (2004, p. 109) states:

> Educational leadership is widely recognised as complex and challenging—and this complexity is difficult to measure. Educational leaders are expected to develop learning communities, build the professional capacity of teachers, take advice from parents, engage in collaborative and consultative decision-making, resolve conflicts, engage in educative instructional leadership, and attend respectfully, immediately, and appropriately to the needs and requests of families with diverse cultural, ethnic, and socioeconomic backgrounds.

School leaders have a distinctive role to play at three different stages of the change process: mobilization, implementation and institutionalization (Fullan, 1991). The initial stage of the reform is a process of mobilization for change. Fullan (1991) suggests a distinct function for leaders during the mobilization stage. School leaders have to develop their own knowledge of the changes and familiarize their staff with the reform program's content. It is important to help teachers and stakeholders to understand the rationale for change. Moreover, one of the functions of school leaders is to persuade and convince hesitant or reluctant adopters to accept and engage in change. In order to provide the requisite momentum, school leaders have to provide adequate resources, support and leadership (Fullan, 1991).

During the implementation stage, school leaders are responsible for creating a feeling of ownership towards goals through participation in discussions, making decisions and setting goals

(Fullan, 1991). Educational reform is a process of change that is continuous and takes a period of time to create and sustain. School leaders can sustain the change initiative by embedding the process in the school system through institutionalization (Fullan, 1991). Furthermore, changes in administrative structure and procedures are necessary in order to support the new institutional practices. Delegating authority to relevant professional leadership at the middle management level or teachers is a practice that has to be institutionalized (Fullan, 1991). Mobilization and implementation are interrelated, in that they occur at the same time, rather than as distinct sequential phases. Also, their order and nature depend on context. Thus, the role of school leaders is complex because they occupy different roles at different stages of the change process. These stages and roles are interrelated and are put into practice according to context.

However, the role of a change agent is not one that belongs solely to the school principal. The literature suggests that leadership should be exercised at all levels of an organization. James and Connolly (2000) argue that a feature of the complex nature of leadership is its ability to operate at different levels, i.e. with regard to the self, groups, and the whole organization. Effective leaders can develop collective leadership in which they engage with their staff by sharing leadership roles, thus encouraging shared responsibility for improvement (Chirichello, 2002). The school principal as an individual can create the conditions, on an organizational level, for leading change through shared and collective responsibility. To unpack this in Qatari context, I ask individual principals and other staff who have leadership roles about their practices and perceptions in leading the change process. Chapters Four through Seven narrate these Qatari leadership stories.

School leaders' roles will include both leadership and management, depending on the context. Indeed, "leadership" and "management" do not always come as a package. According to Yukl (2002), it is obvious that a person can be a leader without being a manager and vice versa. West-Burnham (1997) further distinguishes between leadership and management, arguing that leading is concerned with vision, strategic issues, transformation, people, and doing the right things, whereas management is concerned with implementation, operational issues, transaction, systems, and doing things right. Similarly, James and Connolly (2000) view leadership as involving influence, relationships, people, inspiring and motivating. Management, on the other hand, is concerned with authority, controlling, monitoring and problem-solving. James and Connolly (2000) emphasize that leading and managing both relate to processes, not individuals. In this book, I take an alternative approach to conflate the concepts of "leadership" and "management" by considering that leaders are both leading and managing the process of change at any given moment.

A model to explore leaders' perceptions in Qatar

Educational change is highly complex, as the abundance of academic literature regarding the subject makes clear. A detailed understanding of the intricacies of change management requires an exploration of the nature and characteristics of change itself, for change is not a new concept, nor is the theoretical discipline of change studies a new development within the field of education. This can be deduced from the plethora of interpretive models developed in this domain. Rather than being based on a single pre-existing model in the literature, the conceptual framework for my study is based around one overarching model that I developed using the literature while keeping in mind Qatar's context (see Figure 4).

I consider change as an educational concept by delineating, as in Figure 4, four intersecting strands. The first three vertical strands—understanding change, managing change, and sustaining change—are derived from Fullan (1991), in which he demonstrates the need not only for new ideas but also for understanding and sustaining the process of change. I include the emotional nature of change as a fourth strand because of its prominence in the leadership literature, but also in reference to my data from my previous research, indicating that emotional responses are vital parts of change implementation and deserve further consideration.

The four horizontal themes—resistance to change, conditions for change, change agents, and adopters (Figure 4)—emerged from multiple sources, namely, Ellsworth's model (2000), the literature on change models, my own experience as a Qatari education professional, and the current requirements for National Professional Standards. These four themes represent the areas of greatest potential input from Qatari school leaders. Finally, these vertical and horizontal themes are combined together with the ultimate aim of weaving these themes with the earlier cited general elements of change into one overarching model.

This section's consideration of change as a concept will feature the four vertical intersecting strands: understanding change, the emotional nature of change, managing change and sustaining change. These four strands can be viewed as a consequence of Fullan's (1991) view that both new ideas and understanding and sustaining the process of change are equally important.

Effective leadership involves an integration of what leaders should do (leaders' roles) within the context of change (change themes) through effective use of tools (change strands). The four strands selected are those identified as most appropriate in creating a lens through which to view, consider and understand the ways in which leaders deal with the complexity of change in their own schools, as illustrated in Figure 4. Since I intend to demonstrate the integration of the four context strands in the discussion of each of the four change themes, I introduce the strands first in order to outline background principles before the strands are encountered in the context of each theme's discussion. As depicted in Figure 4, the four context strands are relevant to all the change themes.

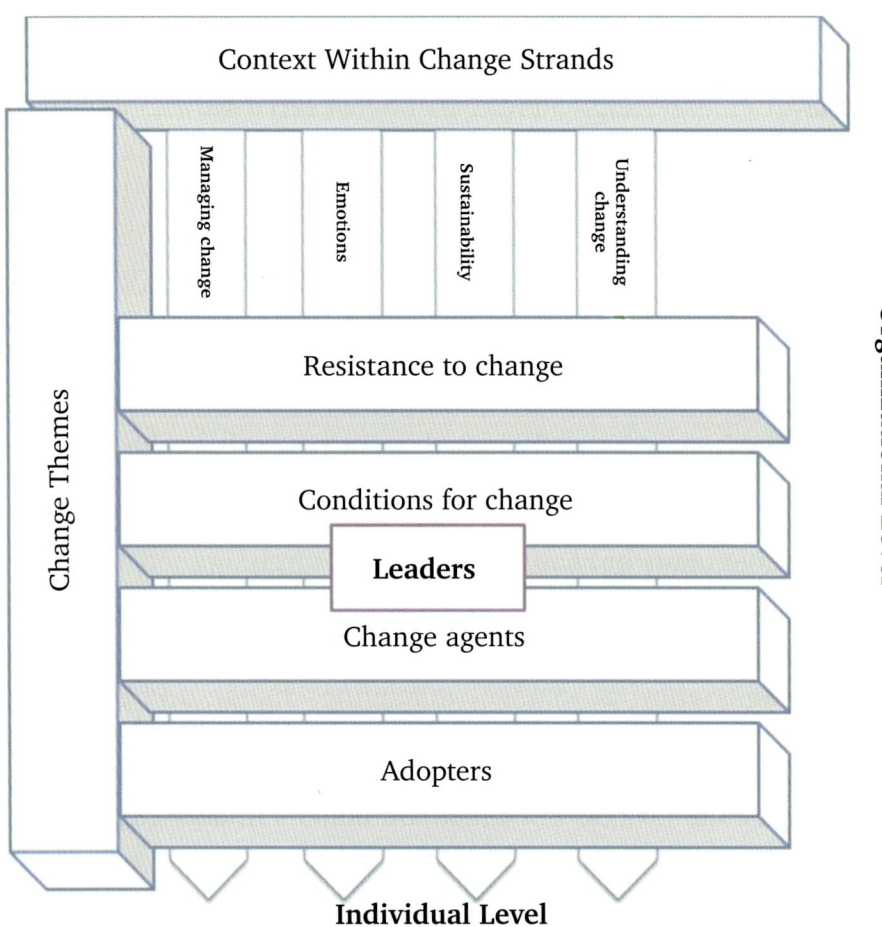

Figure 4. Leaders are at the center of the "change tapestry"

Ultimately, the tapestry presented in Figure 4 will be used in this study as a lens to explore leaders' perceptions of the educational reform in Qatar, both on an individual level (school leaders) and on an organizational level (school level). The four themes and four strands will allow me to focus on those elements of change connected to leadership: management, resistance, and individual and organizational change. The different strands of the tapestry depict change as both individual and organizational. As shown in Figure 4, school leaders are at the center of this tapestry since leaders have a major influence on the change process as indicated in the literature. I used these four strands to develop my interview questions and to guide my observation schedule. This allowed me to focus on exploring leaders' practices in managing the reform and in exploring their views.

Chapter Three

PORTRAITURE AS A METHODOLOGY TO UNDERSTAND THE IMPLEMENTATION OF THE REFORM

In this study, I focus on cohort one and two schools as presented in Table 1. These schools have experienced more than nine years of change under the reform. My goal is to obtain data from schools with the longest experience of change under the reform: I prefer to examine leaders' perceptions of their experiences after sufficient and significant involvement with the reform.

Year/cohort	Boys' schools	Girls' schools	Selected case study
2004 Cohort one	2	4	The case study schools are from cohorts one and two
2005 Cohort two	4	7	
2006 Cohort three	3	2	
2007 Cohort four	5	3	
2008 Cohort five	4	3	
2009 Cohort six	2	3	
2010 Cohort seven	11	12	

Table 1. School numbers per year/cohort

Purposive sampling serves the purpose of my study in order to access knowledgeable people, "as the concern is to acquire in-depth information from those who are in a position to give it" (Cohen, Manion & Morrison, 2007, p. 115). In this study, the participants were knowledgeable about implementing the reform over more than nine years.

At each school, I chose to interview the school principal, two vice-principals (academic and administrative), the four main subject coordinators (Arabic, English, science and math) and a group of three or four teachers from each school to make up the sample (see Table 2). In Qatar, schools are gender-segregated; therefore, the principals and entire staff of the schools match the gender of the student body, male or female. I selected three female schools and one male school. Teachers are followers in that they implement the reform, so interviewing them helped me to gain perspective on leadership practices in each school.

I visited the selected schools between September 2011 and January 2012, spending two weeks in each school. The research design followed three phases of data collection and analysis. The first phase involved initial interviews to gain an overall impression of the school and to obtain more data about the leadership team and their job descriptions. This phase also included non-participant observation and shadowing school leaders to gain more in-depth data about leaders' roles in the change process, specifically how they manage the change, how they deal with conditions of change, and how they build staff capacity to sustain the change process. Phase two involved school-level document analysis and in-depth interviews to gain more qualitative data by identifying leaders' perceptions and practices more precisely, obtaining data that could be used to validate the observation data. Finally, phase three included data analysis and writing a portrait of each school.

I began data analysis during fieldwork, keeping a fieldwork diary to write up any thoughts or items I wished to explore further, as well as to record information as it was revealed. Keeping a diary helped me to record thoughts for further investigation. Although interviews and observation were my main data collection tools, my fieldwork diary became an important tool to determine the categories, relationships and assumptions that informed the participants' views about the educational change.

During observations, I described, then analysed, the events observed to make sense of the setting and interactions between participants. I used the observation schedule to record relationships between participants and others and also between individuals and the school context. During observations, certain themes continually emerged, and the observations enabled successful tracking of those themes. For example, I knew that I could listen to the interviews several times, but with the observations, I was always aware that I could not re-visit the school setting again and that each observation was unique. Hence, I used the observation schedule to help identify themes and questions for further investigation, as well as to inform my focus for the in-depth interviews. For example, I found that I needed detailed evidence of the interaction between the heads of department, and so the next day spent more time in the heads' room and engaged in such observation.

After data collection, I began data organization by transcribing digital recordings and listening to each interview in full before breaking it into parts. All interviews were heard twice for an accurate content orientation before I transcribed them. This process enabled a greater personal closeness to the data and deeper reflection on its content. I transcribed the interviews in Arabic, and then read several times in order to familiarize myself with the responses, before summarizing the main points. I then listed key ideas and recurrent themes from the data in English. I classified emerging themes and highlighted illuminating quotations. I translated these quotations from Arabic into English.

Next, I started thematic analysis by reading through the interview data several times, alongside observations and field notes for each participant and in each school. This focused analysis of their perceptions allowed me to listen to leaders' statements and intentions and then triangulate them with observations of leaders' daily practices in order to come up with a supportable conclusion about what leaders believe and perceive.

My final stage involved the creation of a portrait of each school. I organized my data by breaking it up into short stories within each school, synthesized it, and searched for patterns. This stage of data analysis involved adding my interpretation and understanding of the narrative which had been developed using field notes and observation data.

Cohen et al. (2007) describe qualitative data analysis as a "reflexive, reactive interaction between the researcher and the decontextualized data that are already interpretations of a social encounter" (2007, p. 282). Cohen emphasizes that non-verbal communication gives more information and richness to the data collected; therefore, I added comments on each interview, especially as it pertains to the "visual and non-verbal" (2007, p. 281). I developed a collection of extracts from interview data and field notes organized into themes for each school, from which a skeleton narrative was developed.

Portraiture in qualitative research

Portraiture is a qualitative method for telling the stories of individuals and groups. Sara Lawrence-Lightfoot introduced the concept in her 1983 book *The Good High School: Portraits in Character and Culture*. In *The Art and Science of Portraiture*, Lawrence-Lightfoot and Jessica Hoffman Davis (1997, p. xv) define the portraiture methodology:

> Portraiture is a method of qualitative research that blurs the boundaries of aesthetics and empiricism in an effort to capture the complexity, dynamics, and subtlety of human experience and organizational life. Portraitists seek to record and interpret the perspectives and experience of the people they are studying, documenting their voices and their visions—their authority, knowledge, and wisdom. The drawing of the portrait is placed in social and cultural context and shaped through dialogue between the portraitist and the subject, each one negotiating the discourse and shaping the evolving image.

I adopt portraiture as the main approach in telling the stories of my four selected schools. Inspired by Lawrence-Lightfoot's approach of "[telling] the stories, paint[ing] the portrait—from the inside out", each portrait aims to develop a full picture of the complex realities of leaders whose schools experience change. As seen in Chapters Four through Seven, this is achieved through describing the context of each school and individual, together with leader-staff interactions. Similar to Lawrence-Lightfoot's "group portrait", this study employs cross-case analysis in locating the similarities and differences of each school's portrait (see Chapter Eight). The experiences of school leaders managing the educational reform, leader-follower interactions, events and short stories gathered all lend themselves to portraiture.

The portraits were developed from the data collected at the interview, the field notes, and the observations. My daily field notes and transcripts were regularly examined for signs of repetitive patterns and contradictory data. I sought the roots of any emerging contradictions, while persistent repetitions and resembling patterns were identified and evidence of central themes located. Lawrence-Lightfoot (1983) states,

> Slowly the structure of the portrait would begin to emerge, filled in over time by detailed evidence and direct quotations. At this point the task would shift from solely searching for evidence and distilling themes to one of composition and aesthetic form, from finding the plot to telling the story (1983, p. 18).

The portrait approach has been discussed by many scholars including Hackmann (2002) and Waterhouse (2007). Hackmann's view is that "the portraitist searches for the authentic central story as perceived by the actors within the setting" (2002, p. 54), while Waterhouse (2012), writing three portraits of leadership practice in schools in England, states:

> Portrait is the researcher's construction of a lived, contextual and cultural setting. It is created through a complex series of observations, analyses, interviews, dialogues and critiques of work-in-process. It is a valid representation in so far as it is partial and a product of a unique perspective and a unique set of experiences. (p. 10)

Portraiture has been used as methodology in educational leadership. P. Thomson's (2002) *Schooling the Rustbelt Kids* examines schools in post-industrial cities to identify the changes necessary to ensure children's equal educational opportunities. It features portraiture as a key approach, as does a qualitative study of leaders in twelve schools in England conducted by Day et al. (2000). In the latter example, the team illustrates the ways in which effective school heads promote individuals' development, enhance school relationships, and maintain their focus on goal and program coherence. Despite portraiture's considerable appeal and applicability, it has also attracted criticism. For example, F. English (2000) argues that listening for a story involves the assumption of that story's "real, 'ultimate' meaning, or true identity for an individual and their thoughts". He unequivocally criticizes portraiture's "failure to interrogate what it conceals, i.e. the politics of vision" (2000, p. 21).

Nevertheless, portraiture has been adopted as a central technique for this study because of its written descriptive focus. School leaders are described, through portraiture, as they deal with the challenges surrounding them. This approach goes beyond the ethnographic method of "listening *to a story*" and instead requires the researcher "to listen *for a story*" (Lawrence-Lightfoot & Davis, 1997, p. 13). Each of this study's portraits included an account of my own actions, decisions and reflections to illuminate the data obtained; I posited my interpretations in this way in order to maintain professional rigor. In writing these portraits, an attempt was made to be as faithful as possible to the perceived meaning of the participants. The four school portraits, which are presented in narrative form, are classified with pseudonyms, and so are referred to as portraits of Alnoor, Doha, Aljazeera and Gulf Schools. Pseudonyms were used to maintain the anonymity of the participants in this study.

This study features an account, in story form, of each school from the participant viewpoint, detailing leaders' practices in managing the reform. A detailed description was created through combining data from observations, interviews and documentary evidence. Key themes and patterns emerged from open coding

(Miles & Huberman, 1994). Categories for leaders' perceptions, their challenges and experiences managing change were derived from interactions during the school day (verbal and non-verbal) in meetings and interviews.

Participants involved in the study

As outlined in Table 2, this study's participants included, at each school, the principal, two vice-principals and four heads of department who were involved in the implementation of educational reform. Interviews were additionally conducted with three or four teachers from each department to gain a broader perspective on the reform implementation context. At first, I attended several department meetings, choosing these teachers at random. However, because of time limitations, my choice was subsequently restricted to those participants whose contributions appeared to yield the richest data to be followed up on in the next observation round. This more restricted group focus consequently allowed for a deeper analysis of the data obtained.

Main participants	Informal interview
School principal	---------
Administration vice-principal	---------
Academic vice-principal	---------
English coordinator	3-4 teachers
Arabic coordinator	3-4 teachers
Science coordinator	3-4 teachers
Math coordinator	3-4 teachers

Table 2. Primary study participants

Table 2 shows the main participants in the four schools and the number of teachers in each department. The participants interacted with me in one of two ways: welcoming or hesitant. While the welcoming category straight away cooperated with shadowing and interviews, the hesitant category typically expressed doubt as to their potential benefit to the study. Once I had explained the study to them, their hesitancy soon disappeared, and useful data emerged from their interviews. Only one teacher refused to participate in the study. She had been the math coordinator for the previous year, but had been replaced due to the school's dissatisfaction with her team relationships. These circumstances may explain some of her reluctance.

My role

It was important for me to keep a balance between insider and outsider status throughout the study. A careful balancing of insider and outsider roles was crucial to ensuring that my own interests as an educator did not influence my role as a researcher (Jaworski, 2003). It was important to be detached from events during observations but also to find a way to become involved in informal discussions so as to be able to ask follow-up questions. I was an insider in the sense of having had experience as a teacher and head of department and also in the sense of being familiar with schools both before and after the reform in Qatar. This background gave me insight into curriculum and timetabling matters, as well as a basis for interaction with school leaders and other staff. Also, as an outsider, I was aware of my position as a researcher and the possibility that my views of the school could be overly critical. I guarded against these subjectivities through regular field note reflections.

I tried to balance my role as insider and outsider by being receptive to the ideas of the participants and aiming at a balance between insider knowledge and outsider perspective. I was aware of the potential danger from an exclusively insider status. This perspective could corrupt my data gathering through pre-judgment, or could unwittingly obscure a section of possible perspectives and data. On the other hand, outsider status risks lack of focus due to unfamiliarity.

In what follows, I present and analyse the leadership experiences. I present each school as an individual portrait. These four portraits are created from data collected in four Qatari schools, each of which has nine years' experience of implementing the educational reform and has been led by the same principal since 2004. Each portrait presents leadership practices in managing the reform requirements. In Chapters Four, Five, Six and Seven, I draw on detailed accounts of school leaders and teachers in formal and informal interviews, observations, and numerous field notes. My intention is to draw a portrait of each school in a rigorously faithful way, remaining as close as possible to the participants' own voices.

Chapter Four

FRUSTRATED LEADER IN A CHAOTIC CONTEXT

Alnoor School

Alnoor is a girls' primary school for Grades 1–6 (6- to 12-year-olds). The school comprises around 500 students and around 60 staff, including teachers and administrators. The leadership team includes the principal, two vice-principals and four subject coordinators. The principal was appointed to the school after the reform was introduced in 2004. The school is located a short drive from the center of the capital, Doha, and is comprised of one main building, a sports hall and a separate swimming pool, with an expanse of concrete car parking space in front of the school. The main building with classrooms and staffrooms is two stories high and surrounds an open-air central courtyard, which makes for an uncomfortably hot work environment in the summer.

There are two other buildings, one kindergarten and another preparatory for Grades 7–9 (13- to 15-year-olds). My fieldwork took place in the primary building. The school principal moves between the three buildings, but the other seven leaders all occupy the same building, the primary building. Some of the weekly meetings, workshops and professional development sessions are shared between the main and preparatory buildings, and I attended the two weekly meetings for the management in the preparatory building. One of the challenges post-reform was the lack of school leaders in Qatar. This lack contributed to additional leadership responsibilities as in the case of Alnoor preparatory-level schools managed by a single principal in tandem with a primary school.

The reception area is located at the end of a long walk from the main gate. The doors lead through to a busy area populated by secretaries and administrative staff. Their welcome is warm and efficient. The waiting area nearby is spacious and well furnished, with the school brochure and copies of the recent newsletter available. There are staff on duty to send messages and accompany visitors, and parents are welcomed as they collect their children for various appointments. I attended the school at the end of October 2011, directly before the Eid festival break. At this time the subject coordinators were preparing for tests to be taken after the break. The staff were also attending an external workshop, and in the second week this meant that all of the school leaders had to leave at 10:00 a.m. every day.

Engines of the school: Amna and Mouna

From the moment I walked into the principal's office, I was welcomed. Amna, the principal, first introduced me to the vice-principal, Mouna. Amna sits behind a large desk, neatly arranged with paperwork and computer to hand. The walls are adorned with certificates celebrating honors gained by Amna and the school. A leader in her late forties, Amna has more than 20 years' experience in schools. She welcomes the new reform, explaining: "We all graduated from the old system, but the MoE system doesn't provide sufficient skills for the new generation." Her leadership approach, which is to improve the ability of the staff to cope with the reform, is woven into the everyday life of the school. Vice-principal for administration Mouna has almost 30 years' experience. She projects calm and wisdom, smiles readily, listens attentively and trusts her staff. Her room is businesslike, giving the impression of a place used only occasionally for meetings with visitors. Mouna's real work, it would seem, takes place in the teachers' room and corridors where she can provide support to the teachers. Mouna believed in the reform, saying, "Because I experienced the disadvantages of the MoE system, I'm more convinced by the new system. We were passive under the MoE, but now we have more authority and there is room to be creative. These changes have had an impact on our students' learning."

Amna walked me around the building and introduced me to the rest of the staff. She made me feel welcome by speaking to me in a familiar and open way. She introduced me as a student and a researcher, explaining that I was visiting to learn from them as leaders in the field and to see what their daily experiences were in leading the educational change under the new reform. Amna then asked me to speak about the purpose of my study and how they could help me to achieve that. In my fieldwork journal from that day I narrated this experience:

> I felt comfortable, the whole thing was informal. The staff seemed helpful and expressed their willingness to support my research. They were open in sharing their thoughts and ideas about the positive and negative sides of their jobs. However, the vice-principal asked me to provide a detailed plan of what exactly I wanted to observe and what I wanted to gain from the visit. She explained that the letter I sent through the SEC was not sufficiently detailed. So, this is something to consider and to prepare for the school for tomorrow. It will also be useful for the other schools I will visit. (Field diary, October 23, 2011)

After the meeting and Amna's introduction of my research, the leaders were keen to contribute, offering to help; however, as would become a common theme, they were very busy. They did not ask questions and instead rushed to their classes or meetings.

When Mouna, the vice-principal, speaks of "the engine of the school," she is referring to Amna, the principal. Mouna speaks of her with great respect and deference. Amna and Mouna have been working in this school since 2004 and had also worked together in their previous one. Amna tries to involve her staff in decision-making; however, they always go back for her final word. She is a very committed leader who believes in the idea of the reform, but who expressed disappointment when talking about the lack of support from the SEC. The principal said, "The reform is a good initiative, but the people running it are making our lives difficult." Mouna agreed, commenting:

> Dealing with the SEC is stressful. Some parents are not happy about the new reform, though some of them are satisfied with it. But the problem is once again the SEC and how they treat us. Whether the parents are right or wrong, the SEC always sees them as being right. (Mouna, personal communication, November 2, 2011)

During the interviews I asked about the role of parents under the reform. Amna commented:

> The SEC should think about why parents disagree with the new system, and consider what the real reasons behind their disagreement might be. Instead, the SEC is focusing on how to make the parents happy, doing whatever they can do for them, even sometimes asking us to apologize without giving us a chance to explain our actions. (Amna, personal communication, November 2, 2011)

In my field notes, I wrote: "I wonder why there is a conflict between the parents and the school? Why are there always battles?" Amna's frustration appears in part due to the frequent, unpredictable parent-related demands to which much of her time must be devoted, leaving little time for the vital role of school planning and staff management.

Parents' roles: problems in partnership

During my observations in this school, I did not have the opportunity to see any interaction between parents and leaders or to observe any event held for parents. Hence, I used the school documents available on the school website and as hard copies in order to understand how the school communicates with parents. They have various policies on parental involvement in the school community, and they encourage different kinds of involvement such as membership on the board of trustees or participation through giving talks or reading stories to the students. The school sends a monthly newsletter to parents and holds four parents' meetings every year. Also, parents can contact the school by emails and arrange meetings. The participants emphasized the importance of the role of parents as partners, and this was not possible without support from the SEC.

Despite the number of official ways of contacting parents, some leaders mentioned the way in which parents responded negatively or in unexpected ways to school outreach attempts. A young leader, Maryam, the new science coordinator, who has eight years' teaching experience, is enthusiastic about the change. She confirmed that the new reform gave room for teachers to be creative: "I like the way we teach students to be self-motivated learners, because it's important in teaching students about scientific enquiry. It makes teachers responsible for providing a learning environment in which students can be active and this helps teachers to be creative." However, on the topic of parental support she was less satisfied, saying: "Last year we met with parents to explain the TIMSS (Trends in International Mathematics and Science Study), but the only thing they asked about was how their own girls were doing. They had no interest in encouraging their girls in such an important international test. But in fact we need their support." Reem, a tall woman with a warm smile, a new vice-principal with ten years' teaching experience, expressed similar disappointment in parents' responses: "Sometimes teachers make mistakes in spelling or on worksheets or other tiny mistakes. Parents then come and complain, and I think parents sometimes aren't aware of how they waste our time and effort. The problem is that the SEC has given them the right to do so." Thus, some of the teachers interviewed here indicated their belief and hope for parents to engage more actively and positively in the reform.

Workload and collaboration: implementation pressures vs. pride in achievement

In addition to problems with parents, it was obvious that some leaders felt immense pressure in their daily routines. In fact, two out of the eight interviews ended with the interviewees in tears. One of those whose distress and frustration manifested in this way was in fact the principal, who felt that her efforts to implement the reform's requirements were unappreciated by the SEC. She reported feeling "frustration when being controlled by the SEC", and she suffered from her lack of authority. The second interviewee who ended our conversation in tears was the Arabic coordinator, who was exhausted and overwhelmed by her workload and her responsibilities as a mother. Intense pressure was obviously affecting some leaders' ability to operate efficiently.

Other leaders, in contrast, described their experience with change positively. Mouna said, "I enjoy the change," and Randa, the math coordinator, also affirmed: "I feel pleased when my teachers are able to implement new pedagogical techniques that they've learned from me or other teachers." Her pride in accomplishing things was evident. Maryam said, "I love teaching scientific enquiry." One interesting comment came from Reem: "Miss Amna always gives me the chance to try new things and to take risks." These leaders have positive feelings towards the change and their own leader has created an environment that supports change, allowing and encouraging her teachers to take risks and try out new things—all essential components of motivation for change.

During my visit to this school, two main reform-related obstacles emerged: workload and collaboration.

Multiplied workload

I observed that the leaders' new role involved multiple tasks and intense time pressure. I therefore tried to do the interviews as early as possible in the morning, between 7:30 and 8:30 a.m., before the leaders started to become busy or had to deal with interruptions. The participants confirmed that they felt that they must focus so much on administration that they can't concentrate enough on their students' learning needs. Amna said she could not spend as much time with the teachers in their classrooms as she would like to, and indeed, I found that she regularly had to deal with several different tasks simultaneously. The workload not only seems to occupy their evenings and keep teachers from their families; it also affects their teaching. Aisha, the Arabic coordinator, has difficulty in balancing her responsibilities as a working mother. She reported, "I enjoyed my first two years as a teacher, and then I felt I was not enthusiastic enough." I asked Aisha about why she thought this had happened. She answered that it was because the teachers had too much to do at the same time. Similarly, Maryam reflected, "I love teaching students science and I try to teach them in a creative way, but there are lots of other things that are going on." Most of the teachers I talked with gave the same view. Maha, an Arabic teacher, said, "I teach three periods a day, and now we need to prepare tests and attend workshops as well. We don't have any breaks through the day. It is too much." The new, heavy workload is causing stress for many teachers.

Leaders were burdened with an increased number of administrative tasks due to management and SEC demands for data. Most leaders had been asked to submit extra reports, statistics, and other paperwork, which they found frustrating. Maryam said, "Every year we have new policies and decisions. They change the lesson plans, the books and the yearly plan." Farida, the vice-principal for administration, a young and very active leader, holds a degree in business administration. She reflected on her experience as a student who graduated from an MoE school, expressing belief that the new reform is "a must" for the new generation. She said: "By 10:00 every morning I have to send student and teacher absences to the SEC." This task required time to complete. Nadia, the English teacher, said, "They are always changing the weekly and daily lesson plans," while Maryam stated, "we have to participate in different activities inside and outside the school: we have a student health program, an environmental program, a science research program, a sports program ... there's no end to the activities." Another opinion came from the Arabic coordinator, Aisha: "I'm always having to take work home. I have new teachers in my department and we have a new reading program for the students that we need to implement."

Paperwork and reports are a large part of managing policies and procedures in the school. On the subject of documentation Maryam, the science leader, reported:

> The big problem I have is the administrative paperwork and writing my weekly reports, since I have many responsibilities with my teachers and it's difficult to include every task in the report. I'm also busy with other tasks outside the department and there's no time to write everything up. For example, today I have to attend the workshop at 10:00 a.m. in the other school building, finish the assessment, prepare the students for tomorrow's activity, and check the other science tests. There's no end to it! (Maryam, personal communication, October 31, 2011)

Aisha also started her work experience in the new system, but she would have preferred to go back to the MoE system, saying clearly, "I wish we could go back to the old system." Her argument was that there was a lighter workload in that system. I remarked that she had not experienced that system, and she answered:

> Yes, but I've heard from the other teachers that there wasn't so much pressure and they weren't as stressed. I'm a mother of three children; I don't have any time for my family. Most of the time I have to take work home to finish it. Also, I've stopped participating in any other social events. (Aisha, personal communication, December 4, 2011)

Some teachers believe that the previous system was less stressful for teachers even though they did not work within it, a view that could be due to opinions prevalent within the Qatari teaching community and national media.

This belief, however, stood in direct contrast with those of Randa and Mouna. Randa, the math coordinator, holds a degree in engineering and has 15 years' experience. Well respected by her colleagues, she is an experienced leader who manages her team effectively. She stated:

> I don't think there is a heavy workload. It's 'doable' and the secret is to organize what we need to do. If I'm organized,

then everything goes smoothly. Also, I have to understand exactly what I need to do so I can finish it on time. Then, I can be more productive and implement these new changes more smoothly. (Randa, personal communication, November 2, 2011)

Vice-principal Mouna agreed with Randa, explaining the reason behind staff workload: "I do believe that teachers are not only responsible for teaching. The new reform requires them to participate in different activities in the school, and unfortunately some teachers consider this an extra load for them." Mouna argued: "If anyone complains about the workload, it means they can't cope with the new system and they want to go back to the old system, where everything is ready-made for them. If we want to change we have to accept the workload. Having extra work is necessary for implementing the change." Within the same group of school leaders, perceptions vary: some teachers embrace the extra requirements, believing them necessary for the eventual advantages the reform will bring.

Both the leaders' personalities and their individual perceptions of their new roles influenced their approach to change management. I observed Randa, the math coordinator, for example, to be smiling and calm, and her personality was reflected in the way she led her team. Randa faces difficulties in her department, mainly due to rapid teacher turnover: "I need to spend time training my new teachers." She explained how she dealt with the difficulties her job presented thus: "I have to simplify things, then everything will go well. I have to deal with these new policies step by step. I need to understand them first, then communicate them to my team." She believed in the reform, saying:

> I've taught math in other systems and in other countries and the curriculum standards here in Qatar are excellent in preparing students to be problem-solvers and critical thinkers. We don't just teach them to use fractions but we also teach them how they can apply such skills in their daily lives. (Randa, personal communication, November 2, 2011)

She further commented, "Sometimes teachers have to understand what the change is all about, in order to be able to manage the new lesson plans. The content of the lessons or the subject has not changed; they've only changed the lesson format. It's not a problem for me." Perceptions of the new workload appear to be variable, depending on individual leaders and how much they truly understand what the changes mean.

Factors contributing to increased workload

Several features of the school environment contributed to the newly increased workload, but these may be explained as a lack of training or preparation of staff for the new system, rather than being inherent in the new system itself. Two key factors causing problems in this school were interruptions and lack of planning.

Interruptions

I observed how the leaders and other teachers were running from a class, to a meeting or to a workshop; they were constantly moving. The principal was always interrupted with other tasks. For example, during the interview with the principal, she received two phone calls, and three teachers came to talk with her. She said: "I have to be in three places at once in this school. I have to deal with students, buses, parents...everything." Considering this comment, in my field diary I wrote:

> I think she is too available to her staff so she doesn't have time to focus on her main tasks. There are other staff who can help teachers to solve those issues. But I couldn't figure out from these short conversations between the principal and the teachers whether they could have solved their issues with other staff, rather than with the principal. (Field diary, November 2, 2011)

In this case, she asked them to come back after the interview. In general, she places great importance on being able to see people when they need to see her. During the interview she commented:

"I operate an open–door policy for staff to talk to me about any issues or concerns." Based on my observations and her comments, the main challenge for the principal was interruptions and, possibly, her constantly open door.

Mouna's main responsibility is to help teachers and coordinators with curriculum issues and administrative tasks. However, her overwhelming focus on minor issues and interruptions prevents her from paying sufficient attention to her main tasks. For instance, some staff came to her to ask about coloured ink for printers, organizing student trips, and student forms. This was the case not only with Mouna but also with other leaders, whose job descriptions do not specify who should be doing what. As a result, she takes some of her work home to finish or has to look for a quiet place to concentrate, which is itself a challenging mission.

Reem, the academic vice-principal, was clearly working under pressure, and I observed the following:

> On Wednesday 26 October, at 7:30 a.m., Reem was preparing her weekly report (she is required to include the reports from each department and submit the full report to the principal every Thursday). Two departments had not submitted their reports yet. Obviously this was going to delay her own report. While she was working, a teacher came in to remind her to attend her lesson on the first floor. Mouna also came in to discuss issuing a new procedure for the curriculum. There were many interruptions and she could not focus on her main task, finishing the weekly report. On top of this, she had to attend the weekly meeting in the other building at 10:00. She commented while I was in her office, "even with all this pressure, I'm always smiling—but I might explode at any moment!" (Field diary, October 31, 2011)

In my interview with Reem, I asked her about managing her tasks on a daily basis, and she commented: "Every day I come to the school and write down what I have to do, but sometimes I don't have control over my day, with others interrupting me."

Reem was experiencing a sense of "loss of control." This example makes clear how important it is for the leaders to be able to deal with unexpected tasks, while maintaining the flexibility to continue with their plan and their priorities among their regular daily tasks. Although the school leaders were aware that the new workload was a problem, they didn't seem to recognize the link between the increased workload and recurrent interruptions. It became apparent that another major contribution to workload was lack of organization.

Lack of organization and planning: the reasons and consequences

As described, school leaders at Alnoor must regularly deal with parents as well as requests from the SEC. Every day, they work towards putting in place basic procedures and trying to run the school according to the new system. As a result, the leaders often do not pay adequate attention to core aspects of school administration. One notable example is the lack of clear procedures for student trips; consequently, student trips were one of the issues the leaders spent more than fifteen minutes discussing in their weekly meeting. There was no clarity on who would accompany the girls, where they would go, and who would cover normal lessons while the teacher on the trip was away. Another example observed was the school's lack of basic procedures for effectively chairing and managing meetings. There was no minute-taking, and during the next meeting teachers spent time going over their memories of the main points of the previous meeting. I observed that the school held meetings about creating policies and spent time on this issue, and that they had the necessary documents and forms, but they did not follow them. Amna, who seemed confident that the correct procedures were in place, responded to my question about parents' concern regarding their daughters' safety on school trips: "We have a clear procedure for trips; I showed it to you, it's there! But, hmmm, to be honest we have new teachers who don't follow what's down on paper." The school had held meetings to create policies and spent time on writing procedures, but they did not necessarily follow them. The lack of organization in the administration of the new system made the reform seem much more difficult and onerous than necessary.

As a further example of lack of organization, the school was dealing with the implementation of a new policy. Mouna and Reem met each teacher individually to decode it. Reflecting on this, I wrote:

> It was the end of the school day at 12:00, and an Arabic teacher came to Mouna to discuss the new assessment policy, a new policy that has been a challenge for every department. Mouna invited Reem to join them. I wondered whether a single meeting with all coordinators and teachers would have been more effective and whether it would have saved everyone time. (Field diary, October 26, 2011)

When I asked her about this, Reem said: "It is difficult to bring everyone together; we have to deal with staff on an individual basis." Arguably, better organization would make reform less difficult work. During my visit, I observed the school was participating in different programs internally and externally under the new system. I made a note to ask the leaders about it in their interviews. Their responses varied. Nadia stated, "I'm not against extracurricular activity but it should be reasonable. I believe the students should be our focus, but most of these activities are aimed, instead, at showing outsiders that the school is active." Nadia also added that school participation in these programs was affecting her teaching in the classroom: "Often I go to my class and I'm thinking about finishing these activities. It's too much for the teachers. They have the teaching, professional development or "PD" sessions inside and outside the school, extracurricular activities and their commitments as mothers and members of the community." When I asked her how this could be resolved, she offered: "The solution is to have someone in the school who is responsible for such activities, but not for teaching." Randa agreed: "We have too many activities. There's no doubt about the benefits of such activities but these activities take time and this affects the academic side of the school." In contrast, Reem, the academic vice-principal, thought very differently. She identified an effective school as actively participating in the community. In sum, the perceptions of the new extracurricular activities varied greatly between different teachers, with some staff feeling these activities added yet another unnecessary burden to their heavy workload, while others understood them to be an important part of the reform and a possible contribution to the school and community.

Collaboration: management level vs. department level

Teamwork is a crucial part of the reform. In this school, teamwork functioned well among the leadership; however, problems were present in some of the departments. It was interesting to observe that the majority of the eight leaders had been working together for over 10 years. Farida commented that she had learned a lot due to collaboration with colleagues under the new system in a short time: "Now, if we have a problem with teachers or resources, I can solve these issues more efficiently." On this point, Mouna explained that the reform gave her the opportunity to learn a great deal from the principal, saying,

> I have learned more than I could otherwise have expected to learn during my whole career. Since the reform I have learnt new skills: I am able now to stand and talk in front of people, and I have more knowledge about my job and more skills that can be applied to solve difficulties. (Mouna, personal communication, November 2, 2011)

Nadia stated, "I always enjoyed learning from Mouna in my first few years in teaching; she used creative teaching methods to teach the girls and she actively engaged in trying new ideas in her teaching." Many teachers felt that the reform gave them the chance to learn more from colleagues.

The senior management had a good relationship with the heads of department in terms of support and appreciation. I met with staff from the four departments, who generally commented that they felt "respected" and "valued". For example, Asma, a math teacher, commented, "We have resources available for us and the important support comes from our head. She's always available and values our efforts." Similarly, Dana, an Arabic teacher, affirmed, "We respect and support each other."

There was clear evidence of intradepartmental collaboration, and in my fieldwork diary, I commented on one such example. During a science department meeting, teachers discussed how they could share "best practices" to help simplify the change and introduce it to their teams, thereby simplifying their workload. Hana, a science teacher, mentioned: "It's important for me to work with the other teachers and for us to learn from each other. I'm learning a lot from the more experienced teachers, because I'm new as a teacher." Maryam, the science coordinator, explained how to build a team, saying:

> It took me time to build my team, and sometimes I have to contact them outside school hours. At the beginning it was hard for all of us but now they understand my leadership methods. I have to clarify things for them in order to help them understand the new policy and convince them to implement it more successfully. Of course it's hard to change things that we used to do, but showing them how this can be beneficial for the students can help to convince them. (Maryam, personal communication, October 31, 2011)

Similarly, Randa said:

> Once I understood what I was supposed to do, it made things easier for me. Also, as a leader I have to clarify things for my teachers. If I only give orders, they won't do what they're supposed to do. And that's the reason why some departments are not working well. I have to convince them of the benefits of the change by building good relationships, and that makes things work as a team. (Randa, personal communication, November 2, 2011)

In the Arabic department, Aisha said, "To implement the change successfully, I have to believe in the worth of the change. I have to convince others that it is important and I have to explain it and show them the advantages of doing it. This is the way we work as a team." Farida agreed with Aisha's view: "When I believe in the change then I have the ability to convince my team to implement the new policy." Many leaders saw their role as understanding the reform and helping others to implement it.

All of the eight leaders agreed on the importance of providing positive conditions to enable their teachers to work more successfully. Most of the leaders agreed on the kind of conditions they hoped to provide for their teams. Reem believed that her role was to provide the specific conditions for change implementation, saying: "I have to provide resources, reduce the teaching load, provide space for teachers to work and if they need any information, such as statistics about students with low ability, then I need to provide this to them." Aisha explained: "I could not ask them to do things unless I provided the conditions required for them to implement the change successfully. Otherwise, they would do it, but the result wouldn't be what I had planned." Also, Mouna had the same view: "I provide time and resources, encourage them and reduce the number of tasks they need to do." Finally, Randa emphasized the importance of understanding her team and providing emotional support for them so they could work successfully.

The participants all agreed on the importance of the role of the leader in building a good relationship with the team. Mouna said:

> Changing other people's beliefs and attitudes is hard, and it can't be done in a day or so. It's doable, but it takes time. I've learned a lot from Miss Amna in these last 10 years. In order to help others with the change, we have to choose the right leader to lead the team, so that they can help to transfer positive attitudes to the rest of the team. And this is the key to being successful in changing others and building a team. (Mouna, personal communication, November 2, 2011)

However, although all leaders mentioned the importance of collaboration, their belief in its central role did not appear always to be supported by action. This was the case for example in the members of the English department, whom I met in their meeting room. I had just introduced myself and the aim of my research, and immediately I was taken aback by their openness. They reported the mistreatment and criticism they received from their head. Maha said, "We don't feel supported and appreciated like teachers in other departments." The English teachers were angry when they talked about their difficulties with their coordinator. Enas, an English teacher, said, "she just gives orders," plainly expressing anger and disappointment. The relationship between the Head of English and her teachers had clearly caused anger and hurt feelings, resulting in an unpleasant atmosphere. Although in theory the leader should have a good relationship with their team under the new system, in practice this is not always the case.

In summary, despite the difficulties the leaders were facing at the Alnoor primary girls' school, they were working hard under pressure and trying to manage their daily tasks with enthusiasm and also with ownership. However, the leaders all agreed that they were facing challenges and this could be observed plainly in their daily practices. Workload constituted this school's main problem. However, some participants do not see workload as problematic, rather they view it as a normal phase of successful reform implementation. As a result of the variation of leaders' perceptions, they responded and managed the challenges differently. Workload affected their life inside the school and their family life outside the school. The participants believed that teamwork was the solution to coping with the challenges of the reform. The school works well together on the management level, but could increase collaboration among teachers as well. The need to improve collaboration in the English department was evident through my interviews. The principal, Amna, reported another solution to managing change. She thought that believing in the importance of the change helped people to work in the new system. She said: "People who believe that the change is necessary continue working and supporting the reform. They look positively at the extra tasks, and they work as a team, but others who can't cope with the change just leave." The leaders in general are positive about the educational system. However, there are suggestions that might make the implementation of the reform easier. These include consistency in policies, clear guidelines for implementation, and a reduction in administrative workload.

Chapter Five

A CARING LEADER MANAGING A CONSTANTLY FRANTIC TEAM

Doha School

The school is situated in one of Doha's busiest areas, housing the main hospital, restaurants and stores. I drove to the school along the main road linking the north side of Doha with the city center and the Corniche area comprising most of the government offices and ministries. By 6:30 a.m. the traffic was congested. Most of the participants I met confirmed that they had to leave their houses early in the morning to reach the school on time. Salwa, the principal, told me, "to avoid traffic I have to leave really early, I live far away from the school so I need to leave before 6:15 a.m." A thumbprint registration system for staff only intensified the challenge of getting to school on schedule. Salwa described avoiding traffic as the key to ensure that she got to sign in on time. This school is a new two-story building with a large parking area. There is a big yard to the left of the main building with basketball and handball courts and a running track. In the entrance, on the wall the four pillars for the educational reform were gold-printed in Arabic and in English. The school vision was clearly inscribed on the front wall facing the school entrance.

On the first day, the principal, Salwa, a tall confident woman in her late thirties, welcomed me in the entrance hall, and then I spent 10 minutes in her office introducing my research. She provided a place for me to work quietly if I needed to work without disruptions. She also provided a computer and a printer. Salwa introduced me to Aisha, the academic vice-principal, who showed me around the building and then introduced me to the rest of the staff. She introduced me to the coordinators in their rooms as a student and a researcher, and explained that I was visiting to learn from them as leaders in the field and to observe their daily experiences in leading the educational change under the new reform.

The school has around 800 students in Grades 1–6 (6- to 11-year-olds). There are around 80 teachers in addition to the administrators. Such a high student number means that classroom capacities were often exceeded. On the second floor, the teachers' room was crowded. More than 32 teachers were crammed into a 66-meter square room, where there was no room for their materials. The result was piles of books on the floor. There were eight tables and 12 small lockers in the space, so it was hard to move.

On the ground floor was the library, where students were tapping quietly on keyboards and another group was scanning through the bookshelves. The auditorium and cafeteria were empty during class time. There was a long hallway on the ground floor and an indoor sport hall. On my visit to the school, a teacher was holding a science lesson outside the main building, sitting on the ground under a shady tree. The milder December weather gave the opportunity to teach outdoor topics such as how to grow plants. The school was busy preparing for the National Day celebrations, and during the break, teaching assistants were busy with girls' rehearsals.

The morning I arrived, Salwa, the principal, had just congratulated her team in the morning assembly. She said proudly, "I told them how great they were. They should be rewarded for their team work and for carrying out their responsibilities and I emphasized the importance of continuing this effort." As a researcher who is familiar with the Qatari educational context, I had no problem in deducing the implication (contained in the principal's speech) of previous significant barriers to collaboration. Aisha, the academic vice-principal, subsequently confirmed that the math department was encountering teamwork challenges. She said:

> We have problems between some of the teachers and the departments with working as a team, but having the evaluation people at the school has forced everyone to work

collaboratively, and this is what I'm aiming to emphasize: making the whole school work collaboratively, because we did it last week, so we can continue doing it. (Aisha, personal communication, December 4, 2011)

The school had just finished the evaluation process with the Evaluation Institute (EI)[1], which evaluates each school every three years, and had received the EI report. In the two meetings I attended with the vice-principal and the heads of department, the vice-principal repeatedly emphasized the EI's recommendations for each department.

The principal enjoyed showing me around and was obviously proud of her school. However, when we reached the language lab, she said with disappointment, "we have 200 extra students this year, and we don't have enough classrooms, so we've put the students in the teachers' rooms and we've transformed the language lab into a teachers' room" (Salwa, personal communication, December 4, 2011). They had moved the lab equipment to a distant separate building. The main function of the lab was to help students learn to read English. Maryam, the English coordinator, said: "We had a reading program in the language lab. It was a helpful method to assess reading levels and share reading reports with parents—but this year with the increase in student numbers, we can't use it as before." The current language lab had excellent facilities to help students to learn more effectively, but because of the change of location, this facility and the money spent on it were going to waste. Moving the lab far away from the main building was apparently a tremendous loss. I asked the English teachers if they used the lab. Ameena said, "We rarely use it because it is

---

(1) The Evaluation Institute is responsible for collecting, analyzing and disseminating data and has two primary roles: to inform schools, teachers and students about their performance; and to supply information to parents, to other parts of the SEC, and to other decision-makers on the extent to which schools are fulfilling their roles. This information assists parents in selecting the best schools for their children and allows the SEC to assess the effectiveness of each individual school by implementing an institutionalized system of school evaluation. http://www.sec.gov.qa/En/SECInstitutes/EvaluationInstitute/Pages/About.aspx accessed 10/May/2013

far from the main building and more like an equipment storage room." The lab was full of dust, smelt musty and felt neglected. In total, it took almost two hours to see the whole school.

During the first day, I stopped by a big, clear calendar on the wall outside the principal's office; it showed exact details of professional development workshops, student trips and internal activities. My first thought was that this calendar would be helpful for the structure of my two-week observation. The school aimed to share these events with everyone (parents, researchers, students and others). However, as I spent more time in the school, I found the plan was just for the wall and had no connection to reality. Sudden internal and external meetings, constant change in the school timetable, and SEC-scheduled and impromptu visits rendered the impressive plan useless. My field notes recorded: "I wonder how much time and effort was spent on creating such a detailed and professional-looking calendar?" (Field diary, December 7, 2011)

Countless and varied pressures prevented the calendar plan's implementation. In addition to the external pressures described above, there were internal factors such as managing day-to-day issues, dealing with parents and students, and facing technological problems. Salwa said: "At the beginning of the year, we plan the yearly calendar, but sometimes we do not follow it because of external visits or having to attend external training. For example, last week we had the EI and obviously we could not follow our plan." Maryam also said: "We put a lot of effort into planning our schedule but we need to stick with the plan." Both comments highlight the school's lack of organizational skills. The calendar remained purely symbolic, providing an appearance of organization at odds with the school's actual day-to-day running.

As part of her introduction of me as a researcher to the school community, Salwa sent a staff circular outlining the aim of my research. That was particularly helpful for my observations and moving around the school. One teacher commented: "You are a researcher, you aren't from the evaluation people?!" thus clarifying my role and visit purpose, and emphasizing my lack of affiliation to the EI, which was key to ensuring that those I observed could act naturally.

Principal Salwa: leader as a mother figure

Salwa, the principal, was a very caring leader who was trying to build a family environment. She acted like a mother, patting staff on the shoulder and calling them «ماما» (Mommy or dear). This colloquial expression is used to convey support and to illustrate that they are under her care. In Arabic we usually use this word for daughters as an affectionate term. She perceived that this kind of emotional support was important for team building. I interpreted her use of this term in this way, and she also emphasized it in her interview. She is an energetic and dedicated leader whose personal life and family situation enabled her to spend a great deal of time on her work. In her late thirties, she had a three-year-old daughter. This is fairly unusual in Qatari culture. Since graduation, she has been able to devote her time to the school. She said: "I have one girl, but I still have time for my work and my family, because I have a supportive husband and my father always encouraged me to continue the job I love. I would die if I stayed at home without a job." Salwa was the first principal of the school and she faced enormous challenges, namely the introduction of new curriculum standards, perceived parental dissatisfaction with the reforms, and huge resistance to the reform from both the community and the media.

Aisha was new as vice-principal for academic studies. She was a young leader and enthusiastic about the reform. Aisha's leadership style appeared more bureaucratic. During her interviews, she appeared open-minded and accepting of new ideas from staff. However, during the two academic meetings, she seemed anxious to maintain control. The coordinators could not participate as they wanted, because Aisha talked most of the time. She was quite particular about details and fond of giving instructions to her team. As the academic coordinator, Aisha was given two recommendations from the EI report: first, classroom group work should be increased, and second, there should be more differentiation between students (providing different levels of activities for students based on their abilities). In every meeting with her, I observed that she reminded her staff about these two academic requirements. From the interview, it was clear that she believed that she needed to monitor these requirements. Salwa's personality sharply contrasted with Aisha's. Their partnership worked because in many ways they were complementary. Aisha was more rigid, confident and aggressive while Salwa was successful in establishing an environment that encouraged her staff to thrive—a fact which her staff later confirmed.

Collaboration: good in parts

Seham, the science coordinator, and her sister Samia, the math coordinator, were both working under pressure, because this was their first week in coordinator positions. Seham described the situation: "I know my teachers. I used to be a teacher with them, so that reduces the pressure on me." However, Samia mentioned the challenge of leading a team where one member had been the coordinator of the team before her. She was referring to Fadia, the math teacher, who was now teaching in the department she had previously led. I could not get more information about Fadia since she declined to be interviewed. She did not participate in discussion during the math meetings, and her facial expression conveyed unhappiness. Fadia had been the coordinator in the previous year. The department was suffering from difficult member relationships. Samia suggested that accepting each other's views was important for building the team: "We have to accept each other's views and we have to learn from each other. I have a responsibility to be a good model for my teachers and accept their views, so they can accept my views in return."

In some departments, there was positive collaboration within the team. For example, in the English department, Amal, an experienced English teacher, attended the staff meeting during the absence of her coordinator. Then she communicated the management's instructions to the English department team. It was a good example of the English coordinator Maryam's efforts to build her team's capacities. Maryam said, "I have a good relationship with my team." As she explained to me, "I understand that my teachers have heavy workloads and I have to listen to them and provide support for them." When I asked her how she built her team successfully, she said:

> It hasn't been an easy task. I have dealt with some teachers who worked with the Ministry of Education for a long time and it was difficult for them to change. But it was my responsibility to show them the advantages of the new system and to encourage them when they make any improvements. I demonstrated to a group of teachers two kinds of teaching: the first kind, older-style teaching with no student participation, and the second kind, teaching that focused on the students as active learners. I showed them that the second example was what we need to teach in the new system. (Maryam, personal communication, December 4, 2011)

Maryam added that it was important to build good relationships. She said, "Importantly, I showed my team that I'm not the boss and I don't just send orders to them, because that's not going to work." Maryam was an example of a leader who understood what the reform required her to do; moreover, the other members also had shared some responsibility for building the team.

Maryam, the English coordinator, taught seven lessons per week for Grade 5. Her other responsibilities included supervising teachers and supporting them in their lesson plans, observing their classroom practices and giving feedback. She was a calm person who had a good relationship with her team. I met her in the teachers' room. When I asked the number of people on her team, she said: "I have nine teachers. My teachers are with me in the same office, because I can't leave them, and I have to be with them and available to them so that we can share, talk and help each other. Having all of us in the same office can help to achieve that." (Maryam, personal communication, Devember 4, 2011)

Another leader collaborating well with her team was Basma, the Early Years coordinator, a lively woman in her early thirties, who had arrived at this school when it opened in 2004. When I entered the staffroom, she was printing photos to be attached to students' folders. Basma was also responsible for issuing the monthly newsletter. Although, as a newer graduate, she was enthusiastic about joining the new school system (having no experience of the MoE system), she was also attracted by Salwa's professional reputation and her leadership approach. She confirmed that she had a good team to work with, which was important for having a successful department, saying: "I have ten teachers. At the beginning I was worried about how to work with them, but they work as a team, and for me as a leader this makes many things easier. Sometimes they have issues but we're able to solve them internally." It therefore emerges that, ideally, both leader and team members should actively construct the team dynamic.

Leaders' responses to their challenging roles

This school faced a number of challenges, and participants' responses to these were keenly observed. On the day I had a meeting with Salwa, she was simultaneously carrying out several tasks, some of which could easily have been handled by other staff. Within 10 minutes of visiting Salwa's office, I observed an onslaught of activity. The Arabic teacher entered to discuss student rewards in great detail, asking: How much should the gift cost? Should all grades receive the same gifts? Salwa took the calculator to calculate the cost per student. Then the drama teacher came to discuss the students' National Day activity. A third teacher came asking permission to attend assembly for her son in another school. Finally a fourth teacher came to discuss the medical absence form. Salwa was dealing with many tasks, one after another. From this observation, it is clear that leaders must cope with demands while remaining focused on continuing their plan and overall priorities as a regular daily strategy.

Meeting school leaders in the teachers' room gave me valuable insight into their own strategies for daily challenges. The layout of the room and the piles of folders vividly conveyed these challenges as well. Samia, in her first week as coordinator, came into the room and yelled, "I want to be a teacher again; I don't want to be a leader!" She looked at me and said, "I'm always crying at home. I don't want this position." Samia was eager to leave the leadership role and return to the curricular and pedagogical world of teaching.

Resistance to change

Leading staff is a crucial challenge for the leaders under the reform. Samia said her main challenge was teachers who resisted the change and new ideas. On the same topic, Basma said:

> In response to the reform we had three groups. There was a group of staff who were self-motivated and risk-takers who wanted to try new experiences. They accepted the change and joined the new system, because they had been fed up with the MoE. The second group were those who resisted the change at the beginning, not because they refused the change in itself, but because they didn't want to change what they used to do. The third group were those who resisted and didn't accept the change so they couldn't continue in the independent schools. They left to find other jobs. (Basma, personal communication, December 15, 2011)

Dealing with the second group was difficult. Aisha described resistant staff as "this group [who] don't want to leave their comfort zone. They don't want to change what they are used to doing, what they are comfortable with." Maryam offered the following commentary: "Resisters don't accept the change, because they don't have enough information or skills to implement the change." Salwa said: "I don't deny that we have resisters in this school, but I always encourage them with a smile or a "well done" or any kind of reward. Most importantly, that I have to understand their personality, in order to deal with them" (Salwa, personal communication, December 14, 2011). On managing resisters, Seham said: "I have to listen to the resisters, because as a leader I have to understand the reasons behind the resistance, and then provide solutions." These leader commentaries illustrate their perception of their responsibility to understand resistance to change and to try to manage it by identifying reasons behind it and providing solutions.

Seham was a leader and also had teaching responsibility. Dealing with special needs students was one of her main concerns as a teacher, but she could not find the time and space in her busy and crowded classroom to organize learning activities for those students. An increased student number this year prompted her concern over adequate planning time for special needs students. Seham explained, "I wish I could have more time for special needs students. I have two in my class but they need more time and different activities." When I asked her about the assistants, she said, "We don't have a special needs and learning difficulties specialist. We have assistants in each classroom but our assistants don't have the right skills because most of them only have a high school certificate" (Seham, personal communication, December 13, 2011). Basma confirmed that teaching assistants needed more training not only on working with learning difficulties but also in improving their technical skills. In her interview, she commented that, "I have to know my team's weaknesses and provide solutions for them."

The school has many internal teacher training workshops. There is a workshop every Thursday after school time until 3:30 or 4:00 p.m. Seham stated that the professional development on Thursday was an opportunity to meet with the other staff, since before and after the workshop there was time to talk with teachers from other departments. However, during the week everyone is busy, so attending these workshops seemed to increase teachers' stress. I observed an English teacher arriving at the staffroom straight from teaching three lessons in a row. She was tired and when another teacher told her that the workshop was cancelled she was delighted. A new English teacher then asked whether attendance was mandatory. Another replied: "Yes, we have to, because it will affect our evaluation at the end of the year." The teachers felt that these workshops were simply a pointless exercise and did not see their value and regretted their imposition on an already demanding workload.

Dealing with the SEC's demands: a call for greater flexibility

Dealing with the SEC was a challenge that encroached on school leaders' time. Samia did not have enough time to monitor her teachers: "I want to focus more on my teachers' work and spend more time with them in the classroom, but most of the time I can't do it, because we have to finish the ongoing requests from the SEC." My field notes describe the situation: "Leaders' efforts were shifted away from classroom practices and from the students who should have been the focus of their effort, not the paperwork and filing." Ongoing SEC requests were increasing the leaders' workload. A worried science teacher expressed this thoughtfully:

> There is too much paperwork, and we have lots of files. The time we spend preparing these folders could be used instead to find new teaching strategies and focus more on our lessons. Reflecting on lessons is good practice, but it takes time. Extra paperwork is not helpful but we have to prepare it just as evidence for the SEC. (Teacher at Doha School, personal communication, December 4, 2011).

Another SEC-provoked challenge was what Salwa described as "urgent requests". She said, "Sometimes the SEC requests something and asks us to send it the same day or the following day." Schools do not have a choice whether or not to respond, and this is the reason behind their constant last-minute planning changes.

The school is obliged to follow the new policies, and the leaders have to convince their teams to follow the SEC rules. Samia explained, "It will be for the benefit of students." For the leaders, no matter what it will take in terms of their time and effort, they should implement it. Samia repeated these words in her interview many times: "We have to do this and we should follow that, so we don't have any other choice. We have to convince our team, because it comes from the SEC." Similarly, Maryam said, "We don't have any other choice, we have to do this and we have to follow instructions." Seham also confirmed the SEC's authority: "Even if we disagree with a new policy, we have to follow it because it's from the SEC." Reshma trusted that any changes were for her benefit or that of her students. She said: "These orders were coming from the experts [she meant the SEC] so let's try it. What's the harm in trying new things? We'll know the advantages and disadvantages when we try it." Regarding these responses and practices, in my field notes I wrote:

> After these responses, I was not surprised by their answers about decision-making processes and the meaning of decision-making. With some participants I felt that my question about involving staff in decision-making was quite a strange one to them. How can they be involved in any decision if their role is only implementation and they are only implementers? (Field diary, December 8, 2011)

Basma expressed her frustration that leaders needed to refer back to the SEC in everything. She explained the reason:

> At the beginning of the reform we had more freedom and we did not have to go back to the SEC. But because some school principals understood autonomy wrongly, now the SEC is trying to control this by forcing us to get their permission for everything. (Basma, personal communication, December 15, 2011)

Schools are now "independent" in name; however, in practice, structures of authority seem remarkably similar to the old MoE system. The original aim of the reform was to give school leaders more autonomy, but in the current situation, leaders are only implementers, exactly as they were under the MoE.

Samia, the math coordinator, a smart and a professional teacher, had taught three years in independent schools. From observing the math department meetings, Samia seemed less confident in leading her team. She could not answer team questions, because that was her first week as head of department. As I observed her, I thought that she would be more confident if she organized her day and had a collaborative team. My next thought was how hard it was for her to lead a team in the presence of Fadia, the previous coordinator. Samia invited me to her classroom because one specialist from the SEC was observing her and her use of questions in teaching math. Her 56-meter square classroom had 30 students, arranged in five groups. Having 30 students jammed into a small classroom designed for 20 students was a quite a challenge for the school, increasing teacher workloads and impacting teaching strategies and classroom management. A cramped classroom with 30 students in five groups made it difficult for the teacher and the students to move around and between groups. The reform recommendations stipulated 20 students maximum in each classroom, a limit that the school was forced to exceed.

Not only were student numbers a problem, but the school was facing constant policy change. Samia described the situation: "Every year we have a new policy and I wish I could meet someone in the SEC and ask them, 'What do you want, exactly, from us? What is your strategy or direction?'" The participants experienced the constant change as confusing. Salwa, the principal, differentiated between two types of changes: "Some of these changes are helpful, and they can help us develop our practices. However, some of the changes are not reasonable; for example, lesson plans have changed more than five times during the last three years." All six leaders at this school agreed on the importance of providing positive conditions for their teachers so that they could work more successfully. English coordinator Maryam said: "I should be a link between the teachers and the management. I have to understand their needs and provide support and resources for them." Basma described her own situation: "I have to encourage my team and reward them when they do good work—this is important for them. For example, if they finish their lessons they can leave earlier." Rewarding a team was another type of condition for change. For example, when I was in the science room, Samia came in with a big smile saying that she had rewarded the teachers who had submitted their weekly plan on time with a small gift. Seham said, "I need to do the same with my teachers, they really need more encouragement." As a leader, she believed that rewarding her team was important for building a positive working relationship. Providing resources and rewards, and communicating team needs to the management, are all conditions that teachers need to meet in order to work more effectively.

Buying into the change

Despite the challenges the participants were facing, my impression from listening to the staff and observing their behavior was that they were enthusiastic about the reform and its perceived benefits. Reshma, a Grade 3 teacher, enjoyed being able to use technology in teaching math and science. She said: "We have the latest technology to teach students, and it helps us to implement and facilitate the requirements of the reform." Maryam believed that the reform had positively influenced student learning and also that it had enhanced her professional growth as a teacher and as a team leader. Samia also said that, "the students are enjoying critical thinking and problem-solving activities in their lessons because of the reform." Meanwhile, Aisha believed that the reform provided her with the opportunity to gain more skills and experience.

Understanding new policies on the departmental level was important. Seham believed that it was her responsibility to clarify any new policy to her team: "Understanding a new policy is important. For example, the EI has suggested that we increase our focus on group work this year. It is my role to clarify to my team how to use it more effectively." Also, Salwa said that it was vital that the community understood the requirements of the reform. She seemed to have already accepted the reform. Her clear opinion showed her confidence, uninfluenced by negative media opinions and Qatari society's apprehension about the reform in its early stages. As a principal of a school from cohort one she believed she had a responsibility to encourage parents to uphold the reform:

> We need to educate parents and the whole community about what the new system is about, and what the school needs from them as supporters. I've heard many times from the community and some parents that these independent schools will fail and we'll return to the MoE system. I've always been positive about the reform and I believe in the change. (Salwa, personal communication, December 14, 2011)

However, although participants understood the reform's general benefit, they seemed unfamiliar with, or tended to misunderstand, what it took to implement the reform requirements. There were some problems related to both the implementation process and the implementers. Samia mentioned some of these:

> I'm with the reform, it's a good change, but the problems are with the implementation. On the school level we lack qualified teachers, and regarding the SEC, we can't focus on the students, because we have to respond to the constant requests from them. And the most important factor is that we need professional people to lead the reform more effectively, to make our lives easier. (Samia, personal communication, December 12, 2011)

This school's staff interviews emphasized the SEC's need to understand that the schools' main focus should be the learners, and that teachers should focus more on the students rather than on responding to the SEC's requests. Also, it appeared that school leaders felt they needed clarity regarding new policies. Seham said: "We have instructions from the EI and then we have different instructions from the curriculum office,[1] so we are lost, because the two administrative entities do not meet and agree on one thing." Then she added: "I will talk with the science specialist at the SEC and see what she suggests." Aisha confirmed that they had had different instructions from the SEC units. She said: "They don't communicate with each other. Sometimes we receive instructions that contradict each other. For example, the math people suggest peer work. Then the Arabic unit says we must not use peer work." It seemed that a lack of clear instructions for the school caused a heavy workload, because in order to respond to the SEC unit's instructions, work had to be duplicated. For example, sometimes two different units asked for the same information. In some cases the SEC asked for information in repeated but separate requests, which caused an increased workload for the staff.

The science meeting was held in the science lab; the atmosphere was rather more informal. Seham had a difficult task in trying to convince her team of a policy because it was not clear to her. The school had asked all the teachers to prepare worksheets for different levels (A, B and C) to differentiate between students. Shebanna said, "But we have the book already. Do they need us to do another worksheet that is different from the book?" Sarah said, "They asked us to do that but in the national test they give questions for one level only. That's not logical." Observing this discussion, confusion in the instruction process was most evident both to the leader and to the teachers themselves.

Substantial work(over)load

I had planned to meet with the science department on the second day. On that day, in the morning, Seham was busy with Aisha

---

(1) The curriculum office is one of the four offices at the Education Institute. It is responsible for developing national curriculum standards in key subject areas in order to facilitate high standards of teaching and learning, and for monitoring, advising and supporting schools in the implementation of these standards. http://www.sec.gov.qa/En/SECInstitutes/EducationInstitute/Offices/Pages/CurriculumStandardsOffice.aspx accessed 10/May/2013

and she told me she would come in five minutes. In this school's context, five minutes can routinely signify half an hour. While I was waiting, I realized that some teachers were tired and overloaded. I noted:

> I went to the science department on the second floor, and before entering the room, I saw Layla, the new teacher, sleeping on her desk. It was good that the wall of the office was made of glass so I could see what was happening inside. I felt sorry for her because she was in a deep sleep, and I could not enter the office. I waited outside for a few minutes until another teacher, Shebanna, came by and then we entered together. Then Layla woke up and she tried to continue her work. I pretended that I had not seen her. Shebanna said: "Poor Layla, you have to work hard in this school!" (Field diary, December 5, 2011)

Sleeping behind their desks, running between meetings, and constantly moving between classes all indicated that staff were overloaded not only mentally, but also physically. Fortunately, Seham came back after 10 minutes and introduced me to her teachers. The meeting lasted for 30 minutes; they talked in general about their work and the difficulties they were facing. At the end, Shebanna said, "I feel better when I talk to others about our workload, because I worked in another private school and it was not stressful like it is here." This remark demonstrates how Shebanna's workload affected her emotions. I also observed how teachers were constantly rushed to an unsustainable degree. For example, I found most of the staff did not use their 45-minute break to have time off, but used it to go on with their work. Some teachers tried to have a cup of tea but they always left it on the table, and later they could not drink it because it was cold. This happened frequently throughout my observations. At the end of the day they were tired because they had not had a real break. The shorter breaks and prayer time were occupied with supervising students, answering students' questions, setting up equipment and moving from one end of the building to the other. Excessive workload also affects the working relationship with other departments. Samia said: "We can't share teaching and learning practices with the other departments, because we're too busy with our own stuff. Sometimes in the external workshops with the math teachers we share best practices. But inside the school we don't have time." All the teachers confirmed that they took work home to finish. So the workload seemed to have a negative impact on staff collaboration with others inside the school.

Some teachers found the workload varied considerably. Samia said:

> The workload is not the same in all schools. A friend of mine in another school teaches three grades—3, 4 and 5—so she has only 20 lessons per week. We have loads of folders and papers to prepare, and all of it is evidence for the SEC. We show them these folders when they come. But they could simplify things and ask for electronic copies. The problem is that they ask for the same documents from different people, or different people in the SEC ask for the same evidence. For example, when we had the EI last week they asked me for a document and they asked a teacher for the same document. I explained to them that they already had it in the same folder but they said they wanted two copies. (Samia, personal communication, December 12, 2011)

Seham explained the reason why there was a heavy workload in this school. She said: "We have a heavy workload in this school. And it is different from one school to another. My colleague who left the school confirmed this to me. I think this is because we are a cohort one school and we are aiming to achieve more. That's why we have more work to do" (Seham, personal communication, December 13, 2011). A cohort one school refers to those institutions having started the reform in 2004. Similarly, Salwa agreed that, "We always have a high workload, because we aim for the best, so we put pressure on our teachers!" This was the opposite of what I had assumed, because cohort one and two schools are supposed to have policies in place as they started early with the reform, but in fact, even after nine years of implementation of the reform, more work is expected from teachers. I observed how the Arabic coordinator and her team were stressed by the SEC specialist visit. I was not granted access to that meeting, but I observed that teachers were busy preparing folders as evidence for their work for the specialist. They also changed their schedule, which caused more frustrations and stress. At the end of the day they went to their classes, but the coordinator stayed with the specialist until the visit was over. I could not meet the Arabic coordinator because she was busy inside and outside the school, so I did not include her in my study.

However, the workload was not the same for everyone, or was at least perceived differently by different staff members. An IT teacher, Bara, believed that this school was not overloaded compared with her previous experience. During my visit, I observed that the school had just started implementing a new system for assessment as a requirement from the SEC. Teachers had to use an Excel spreadsheet to record student grades. In order to complete this task, teachers needed Bara's help—so there was no way to avoid spending time talking with the IT person, Bara. I went to Bara's office, and I found that more than five teachers had come to her office at the same time asking for her help. In addition, she had to finish other tasks for the management. Clearly she was stressed and I spent time observing what was going on. At the end of the day, I managed to have 10 minutes with her when she was free from the teachers. Salwa's leadership style, characterized by listening to her colleagues and providing support, made a difference in reducing the heavy workload. Bara confirmed this, saying: "I have lots of work in this school, but compared with my first school, here we have more of a family environment and the management provides support for us to work more smoothly. I try to prioritize tasks accordingly so that I can finish my work and support the teachers" (Bara, personal communication, December 13, 2011).

In seeking to encourage and provide support to teachers, Basma recognized the need to help her staff and set the tone and spirit of collegiality. After the Early Years department meeting, I had a chance to talk with Asma, the math teacher. She said: "We have more burdens on teachers now. We have to prepare a daily lesson plan, which is time-consuming. We have to prepare projects, peer work and extra activities." When I asked her how she was managing that, she responded: "It is at the expense of our personal and family life. I have to work at home and until late at night. I am not saying I have not gained more knowledge and experience, but the time is the factor." Asma confirmed Bara's point that having a supportive leadership can minimize teachers' stress. Asma said: "We have a supportive leader and a collaborative team. Thank God! Without that I couldn't survive." Salwa believed prioritizing their tasks and time management were the best way to manage the workload. She commented:

> I agree we have a heavy workload. But we have to organize ourselves and our tasks. Sometimes I have a plan but I can't follow it because I have to deal with different requests at the same time. Then I have to prioritize: I do the urgent task first, then the important ones and finally the things that can wait for a few days. (Salwa, personal communication, December 15, 2011)

Based on interviews, it appears that staff in this school feel managing workload on the individual level can be achieved by managing their time. Workload varies from one school to another. Workload also varies from one member of staff to another. Some teachers and leaders can cope with their tasks, while some are stressed about them.

Emotional response to change

The working environment can affect the emotions of the staff. During my visit, I have noticed that they use their mobile phones inside the school to communicate with each other. In this school, although they had a telephone in each room and office, they still called each other on their mobiles, due to urgent and sudden meetings and events. Most of the meetings planned and arranged on a weekly or monthly basis were cancelled. When I was with the science coordinator, she suddenly got a message from Aisha asking for an urgent meeting. It was as if they were in the emergency room, and could be called at any time, which created a highly pressurized working environment. Salwa said:

> I did not like the routine and how we taught in the old system. I was always trying to find innovative ideas. Most of the teachers used to teach only in the classroom. But I taught my students in the school garden and in the library, not only in the classroom, because I was always looking for creative ideas. I was always searching for new experiences. I taught PE when we didn't have a PE teacher, I worked in the library, and all of that added new experiences for me. And then when the reform was introduced, we believed in the change and that had a positive impact on our work. We've worked hard from when the reform started until now. Do you know why? Because we chose to join these schools ourselves—we chose the hard work. (Salwa, personal communication, December 14, 2011)

Salwa's attitudes towards the reform had had a positive impact on her work. Even though she was working in a stressful environment, as a leader she was trying to provide support for her team and to reduce the pressure.

There were other examples of how leaders perceived the reform requirements and how they could affect the implementation of the reform. The science coordinator, Seham, had many tasks inside and outside the school. She was teaching Grade 6, leading a team, and a master trainer for new teachers at the SEC. Seham said: "I go [to the SEC] twice a week, one day to prepare for the session and another day to train the teachers. This training lasts for 15 weeks. It is a heavy load for me, especially because I spend time at home preparing for each session." When I asked her about this experience and how she was managing her tasks, she said:

> It is a challenge for me and I am stressed about it, but it adds a lot to my experience. I will use this experience in training my teachers, especially the new ones. I was nominated for this position by a committee from the SEC, who came and observed my lessons. I did not ask if the SEC would provide a wage or not, but for sure it will help my professional growth. (Seham, personal communication, December 13, 2011).

Financial incentives were not her main motivation. Self-motivation helped the leaders to manage their load and cope with the negative emotions that were brought about by the reform.

Ultimately, Doha School has a caring principal who is trying to build a family environment among the staff. Principal Salwa's personality sharply contrasted with that of academic administrator Aisha. Their partnership functioned due to its complementarity; Aisha was more rigid, confident but aggressive, while Salwa was described as successful in establishing an environment that encouraged her staff to thrive. All the departments work well together and they support each other. However, the math department seems to be encountering challenges in its member collaboration. The math coordinator, Samia, is a new and less confident leader who needs time and experience to lead her team more effectively. The school's current barriers to the reform's implementation include: workload, resistance to change, accommodating the SEC's multiple demands, and constant change in the school policies. Despite the challenges the participants were facing, my impression from listening to the staff and observing their behavior was that they were enthusiastic about the reform and its benefits. Nevertheless, although participants understood the reform's general benefit, they seemed unfamiliar with, or misunderstood, what it took to implement the reform's actual requirements.

Chapter Six

AN ISOLATED LEADER FACING VARIABLE STAFF COLLABORATION

Aljazeera School

It was a perfect day to start my visit to Aljazeera School: cool and partly cloudy weather, late December. On the right-hand side was the entrance most often used by students. I entered through the central door. As I faced the main building, there were several steps leading up to a glass door that entered into the reception. Inside the central office was a comfortable waiting area with couches and chairs, and a friendly, accommodating receptionist who welcomes visitors. The school secretary sat behind highly decorated partitions close to the door of the principal's office.

The school is located in the capital, Doha, and has around 500 students in Grades 1–5 (6- to 11-year-olds). It has 75 teachers in addition to the administrators. Aljazeera School has a well deserved reputation as a cohort one school, but that was not the case when the school was opened eight years previously. Kawla, the principal, explained: "When we started we faced a challenge from parents in accepting the idea of the reform, but now they fight to get a place for their daughters."

Kawla and Lwloa: management styles

I met the school principal, Kawla, in her office and she introduced herself informally. A relatively young leader, she started her career as a PE teacher. She introduced me to the vice-principal, Lwloa. Lwloa, a tall woman in her late thirties, had 16 years' experience. She started as an English teacher, became an English coordinator and finally the vice-principal in 2008. Kawla and Lwloa had a close relationship, having been friends and colleagues for most of their professional lives. Before coming to Aljazeera they both worked at Doha School. They are a pair, read each other's minds, and have a kind of understanding that reflects a deep trust between them. Kawla is clearly the big boss, but Lwloa is her committed right-hand supporter. Both women are energetic and have a lively humor that appears privately and during after-school hours. Their laughter and storytelling behind the scenes seems to fuel them for the toughness that shapes their projected professional images during school time.

Lwloa and I were in the same secondary school, so we shared stories about our school days. Kawla focused more on organizational details, rules and regulations, whilst Lwloa concentrated on people's development and learning. Although Kawla wants to be involved in every aspect of her school, she is not around the school often, spending most of her time in her office. Kawla introduced me to her team in their rooms. She also sent an SMS (Short Message Service) to the whole school informing them of my presence as a researcher collecting data about their practices.

From my observations, I found that Kawla was absent from general school activity, spending most of her time in her office. She explained her wish to be more available to her teachers, but administrative tasks she was unable to delegate prevented her from doing so. Kawla said:

> This week I couldn't go to the classrooms or the teachers' rooms. Normally I do, but this week has been a busy week. I don't like to sit in my office. I want to be close to my teachers and be available to them. They are not used to doing things unless they check with me or Miss Lwloa, this is the way we work. I know it is wrong, but I need to know the big things and at the same time the tiny issues in the school. This will protect me from parents' complaints or questions from the SEC at any time. I need to know everything in the school because they will not forgive me if I say I don't know. This is a challenge for me and it is very stressful. (Kawla, personal communication, December 20, 2011)

One example of Kawla's focus on details that could have been delegated to other leaders occurred during my observation of Reham, the English coordinator. I observed the principal asking Reham about joining her teachers on a student trip. I asked her about finding teachers for the trip. She said:

> The principal came in this morning because none of my teachers who teach Grade 3 will be able to go on the trip. One teacher is on a workshop outside the school; another teacher is with her son in hospital; and the third has just come back from a two-day absence and she has had an infection in her shoulder so she can't go. (Reham, personal communication, December 19, 2011)

This example indicated a lack of clear school policies, demonstrating the leader's strategy of volunteer-searching rather than having a transparent policy.

While I was shadowing Kawla, she spent one full morning until 12:00 entering teachers' personal data such as the staff names and ID numbers with the IT technician for the professional license for the SEC. In addition, when the school had a visitor from the SEC curriculum office, Kawla spent almost three hours from 11:00 a.m. until 2:00 p.m. discussing the folders submitted by the subject coordinators to the visitor. As the subject coordinators were also in the meeting, she did not need to be there.

Lwloa was attracted by the new school system post-reform, which provided for her an escape from the routine of the MoE. For 10 years, she had been an English teacher who had tried to be an innovator, but the system did not help at all. When the change was introduced, she knew it was time to pursue another option, saying:

> I joined the independent school because I didn't want to continue with the old routine in the MoE system. Two teachers from the school had joined the new system and liked the idea of the independent school, and then they encouraged us to join. It seemed like a "great adventure" for me. (Lwloa, personal communication, December 26, 2011)

She added:

> I'm with the new system 100%. I'm working in the new system and I can see the difference. Also I can feel the difference as a mother who has two sons. One has been with the new system from reception and now he is in Year 6, and his performance is much better than that of my other son, who joined the system late. This might be because the boys themselves are different, but of course the school environment is an important factor. (Lwloa, personal communication, December 26, 2011)

Ida, the English teacher, agreed with Lwloa on the reform's benefits to learners: "We use learning by doing. Students learn best when they are actively involved in something and this is how we teach under the new system. Five years ago the students' level of English was poor but now they speak perfect English." The new system was seen as focusing on the student as an active learner. Similarly, Nuzhat, the science teacher for Grade 5, had teaching experience in international schools in Qatar and Saudi Arabia and agreed that the use of English as a second language has improved under the reform, commenting:

> I was worried about using English to teach science, but when I came here last year and taught Grades 4 and 5, I was impressed by the students' level of English. It's the same as the international level. Of course some students in each class have difficulties in understanding science in English and this is normal, but I can say 90% are perfect. (Nuzhat, personal communication, December 26, 2011)

Kawla and Lwloa's enthusiasm for reform was transmitted to the English and science departments, which seem to have fewer problems than other departments. However, math and Arabic appear to encounter difficulties relating to the reform's implementation. Rasha, the math coordinator, had staff shortages and workload issues. She received support from the English coordinator, while Raesa, the Arabic coordinator, received support from the vice-principal. Kawla and Lwloa's leadership style worked well with experienced teachers, but it was not so effective with inexperienced teachers. The personality of the coordinators helped the science and English leaders to work well. In the Arabic department, no one wanted to be the coordinator. Raesa was the only option, so they supported her, but this support seemed more emotional than strategic.

At the school level, the vice-principal insisted that all the staff were working well together, commenting:

> We all feel like a family. We support each other. Most of us are leaders who have been working here for more than five years. We have a reputation in the community so we have to keep up the hard work. I tried to resign twice for different reasons, but having a supportive team with the same vision convinced me to change my mind. (Lwloa, personal communication, December 26, 2011)

English and science departments: progressing well

In Aljazeera School, I observed the English and science departments working well. The experience and personality of the coordinators helped them to cope with departmental problems. The English department enjoyed stable leadership. Reham, the English coordinator, was a confident leader who had a good relationship with her team. All her teachers pointed to her personal qualities and leadership approach when they were asked to identify the secret of their teamwork. One English teacher explained that "Reham encourages creativity and also allows people to make mistakes." Reham said:

> I always show my team that I'm available for them when they need me. This gives the teachers confidence in coping with all these changes. I also provide support for them, especially when we have to implement a new policy. I try to reduce other tasks. And the most important point is to consider their other personal issues or problems. (Reham, personal communication, December 19, 2011)

Reham is proud of her work at Aljazeera. She is thoughtful, focused and excited when she talked about the educational reforms. She said:

> I did not work in the MoE system, but I experienced it as a student. For sure, the new system has improved teaching strategies. It has also improved the students' level of English. We have teachers with different experience and backgrounds, which benefits student performance. Students learn science and math in English. This has improved their use of the English language and at the same time, it has helped to improve teachers' knowledge. (Reham, December 19, 2011)

As a leader, Reham provided some of the conditions to facilitate change, but as an implementer she also needed support. She said: "I consider my teachers' issues and try to help them, but at the same time I need committed teachers who do their work in a professional way, because quality matters." Similarly, Rasha, the math coordinator, said: "I need the school to take into account my psychological circumstances, because under all this pressure we need to be encouraged to move forward and we need appreciation." The English department has a supportive leader, and the teachers work cooperatively. Ida, an English teacher, described the situation this way: "We share our teaching strategies. If I learn something in a workshop or I come across something new, I always come and share it with my team such as how to manage the classroom or how to teach creative writing."

Shadowing Reham, I observed her handling of lesson coverage. Teachers refused to take extra lessons, presenting leaders with a challenge. This issue was discussed in the English department meeting. The teachers were complaining about covering lessons, but Reham was positive and tried to provide solutions. After the meeting I talked with Samia, who was also positive. Rafeea, however, had a more negative interpretation of the challenge and complained. I wanted to understand more about their divergent views. Rafeea said: "….covering lessons adds to my stress. I can't just go to a classroom without preparation. I need to plan in advance for a class which normally I don't teach." In contrast to this view, Samia offered: "I teach Grade 3, so I prefer to cover lessons in Grade 3. It is difficult to cover other grades, but we can find solutions for that. I mean we can have general lessons that can be taught to Grades 1 to 3, then another plan for Grades 4 and 5 so we can teach these lessons."

However, Reham, the English coordinator, facing the same challenges, believed involvement in decision-making to be a problem in the school:

> We have disorganization and miscommunication. Sometimes we have to respond at the same time to the management, the students, and the requests from the SEC. This is too much. Pressure can generate innovation but sometimes it generates explosion! The management sometimes ask for urgent things but we can't do it within the time we have. And when we say no, they think that we're resisting. For example, two days ago the management asked us to provide our extra-curricular activity plan. We had submitted this a long time ago at the beginning of September. Now they have asked us again we are doing double the work. But they asked us to put it in a different format, which they still had not sent yet. We need to communicate more. (Reham, personal communication, December 19, 2011)

Interviews with other participants confirmed they all had to deal with resistance when implementing change. Kawla expressed her need to choose coordinators carefully who motivate teachers who resist. She remarked: "We have teachers whose hobby is to say 'no,' and resist everything." Reham recounted her way of dealing with resistance when she wanted to implement a new policy. She said:

> The first step is to convince my team about the new policy. We have to do it anyway, so we have to accept it. Let's find a way to accept it. I have to be positive; if I'm positive then

I can influence my team. I'll still have difficulties but at least I can change the minds of a few members who can help me to implement the new policy. (Reham, personal communication, December 19, 2011)

Reham believed that they would implement the change anyway. The problem was not whether to accept the change or not, but to find a way to implement it. The English teachers had the opportunity to share and discuss ideas with Reham. Ida, with 25 years of experience inside and outside Qatar, commented after the English meeting:

Whenever we discuss anything with our coordinator, we come to a unified conclusion. They give us a chance to contribute. For example, in today's meeting, they wanted us to teach the cover lessons, but we needed to prepare and we needed to finish our own work. They don't just say you have to do this and this, because it's not possible to work like that. (Reham, personal communication, December 19, 2011)

I observed that Reham was a leader who was most willing to share her experience and professional observations with me. This was invaluable to gaining a more detailed picture of one leader response to implementation challenges. Reham's enthusiasm and availability to me as a researcher served to contrast with Kawla's much more limited availability.

The science department's leader, Sarah, a very caring leader in her late forties with 25 years' experience, came to Qatar 25 years ago. The first impression I had of her was that she felt at home and comfortable in the wider community. Sarah was available to her teachers, and seemed to have a good relationship with her team. Before the mothers' meeting [1], Sarah met with the team for 10 minutes. She made herself accessible to give advice, especially to the new teacher, Amani, who expressed her fear of facing the mothers for the first time. Sarah said, "If you need me I'll be

---

(1) Mothers' meeting: Qatari girls' schools normally prefer only mothers to attend school meetings, although fathers may make other arrangements to contact teachers.

there, just try to stay cool. Don't blush; everything will be fine. Just be calm." This kind of emotional support to her team facilitated coping with the difficulties for a new teacher who was not feeling confident about the mothers' meeting. Sarah believed that her role as a leader was important in facilitating change. She said:

> It's my personality; I can convince my team by showing them the positive side of any change. Sometimes they are annoyed and overloaded, so I can change my plan of action. But when we have a deadline it's difficult, because it is out of my hands. What I can control is how I put it to them. I know and I am confident that my teachers will give me the work and submit it on time. (Sarah, personal communication, December 25, 2011)

Sarah also agreed about the benefit of the reform for her as a leader and as a teacher. She said: "I was computer-illiterate when I started working here, but now I am confident about using the latest technology."

According to Nushat, the science teacher for Grade 5, another advantage of the new system is that it makes science relevant to learners' daily lives. She said, "We teach science in a way that can be linked to students' real lives and this is important in learning science, and it's the best way for students to learn."

Nushat explained how she felt before joining the independent school, which contrasted with her opinion once she joined the school. She said:

> I was a bit nervous, but when I met the team and the coordinator I was satisfied, because things were not as difficult as I had been thinking. Slowly, slowly I started learning about the system. For example, lesson plans are quite different here. In international schools where I was working, we used to do a weekly plan. But here we have to do a daily lesson plan. It was a tough task for me, because every day we have to write a detailed lesson plan with timings. At the beginning this was tough, but now it's really helpful. I mean, if the

whole week plan is ready, if I am absent, any other teacher can teach by using the detailed plan. (Nushat, personal communication, December 26, 2011)

Raesa also believed that the reform was a positive change for every learner: "The reform creates a new learning environment in which every learner can have the opportunity to achieve his or her best. The talented students and those with learning difficulties have equal opportunities to learn." Raesa's problems in team leadership derived both from her team members and from her own personality. Having graduated only the previous year, she was too young for the position. She wanted to please her senior management who had no other choice but to choose her for the role.

While the reform aims to create a stimulating learning environment for every learner, teacher quality is key. Yet the principal, Kawla, had a different opinion: "We teach students for the test. I know this goes against the spirit of the reform, but it is a fact that we are forced to do this. We prepare the students for the national test and for the school tests twice a year." She believed that they prepared students to pass the test and not to be lifelong learners. This significant perception coming from a school principal highlights a notable discrepancy between the reform's design and its implementation.

Arabic and math departments: reform-led struggles over collaboration and workforce shortage

I was waiting in the peaceful area near to the principal's office for my meeting with the principal. Raesa, the Arabic coordinator, came into Lwloa's office full of disappointment, complaining about the teachers on her team who were not cooperating with her. Then they both went to Kawla's office, but I did not join their meeting, feeling their need for privacy. Lwloa said to me: "If Raesa wants us both together that means she has a big problem." It was clear that Raesa faced teamwork problems despite leader support. In the teachers' room, Rasha, the math coordinator, also struggling with her team, had another supportive colleague, Reham, the English coordinator. Rasha complained about her difficulties in dealing with one teacher. Reham suggested she send a formal request to which teachers would more likely respond. Rasha seemed very tired and stressed. In short, from day one, the school's obstacles to successful collaboration were clear to me, specifically in the Arabic and math departments.

Raesa, the Arabic coordinator, a newly graduated leader in her early twenties, was a leader for a team of seven teachers in her department, most of whom had more than 10 years' experience. She was a young and inexperienced leader receiving insufficient support. This situation was highly stressful, and indeed, no one wanted her job. She started as a teacher, becoming a coordinator three months prior to my visit. Her challenges stemmed from a less than cooperative team, a fact she mentioned in her interview. This situation was confirmed by Lwloa. The lack of cooperation was also made clear in the meetings I attended with her team. She tried, for example, to make a suggestion about lesson coverage, but two teachers protested and rejected her suggestions. She also tried to change her lessons to attend a meeting, but no one provided help. She found her staff resistant to everything she proposed. Raesa did not want to disappoint the management who were providing support for her. She said, "No one wants to be a coordinator, but I don't want to disappoint Miss Kawla (the principal), so I took the job. The other teachers rejected this position, because it would have added a lot of pressure for them. It's a stressful job, and also the team doesn't work well together." Asma, an Arabic teacher with more than 15 years' experience, described the situation, which was causing emotional problems. She said:

> Every few months we have new policies. We have a heavy workload. I am always stressed and under pressure. I have four children and I can't find a balance between my responsibility as a mother and as a teacher. I've become too nervous and stressed because I don't like to talk with people outside

the school. I was also losing my hair because of the stress. I've become isolated and I need time to be alone and rest. (Asma, personal communication, December 20, 2011)

Raesa was struggling with her team when I observed the Arabic meeting. She had explained to them that they needed to prepare for the national tests. Asma's response was angry: "Tell the SEC we are spending more time on paperwork than on the students." Raesa described her struggle to lead in her interview: "My team doesn't listen to me, so I go to Miss Lwloa and she sends an official request to them. This is the only way that they can respond to me."

Rasha, the math coordinator, had a negative view of the implementation of the reform. She said:

> It's all about working on paper. Everything's all about documentation. As a coordinator and as a teacher, I spend most of my time documenting my work. We used to work to one format for the lesson plans, and now we have a new one. The changes don't help us. We don't have clear policies. Most of the instructions are unclear, and the reason is that the people at the SEC are always changing and when a new person comes in, they send out new policies. They don't look at what was done before and find out what works, they just start from the beginning again. In the end we are the victims. (Rasha, December 18, 2011)

Rasha added: "I'm working under pressure and so stressed, because one teacher is on leave and I don't have enough teachers." Then she laughed in an odd way, and I could see the tears in her eyes. I heard Rasha say to Reham: "I wanted to stay with my husband after his surgery but I couldn't, because all my thoughts were about the department." However, at the end of my visit to the school, she had managed to employ a new teacher, so she was pleased and seemingly less stressed. Staff shortages had previously resulted in extra workload for Rasha and her department.

Reasons behind workload

The testimonies below provide several explanations for the high workload that plagued both leadership and staff in Aljazeera School. The participants need to maintain high standards because they are a cohort one school, which pressures the school to participate in the SEC activities. Kawla described the burden:

> It is assumed that in cohort one, our students have already met specific standards. I feel we are bound to the institution we belong to, and we have been told that "Aljazeera" is always on top. We met the standards, and we have to go even higher than that. The SEC asked all the schools from all the cohorts to participate in the science research program, so if you were in my position would you back out? (Kawla, December 20, 2011)

Kawla felt that the school's position and reputation in the community required them to participate in all the activities introduced by the SEC. The principal also explained that being a cohort one school affected their relationship with parents:

> We always face difficulties in student admissions. Parents want to register their daughters in our school because of our performance and reputation as a cohort one school. But we have rules we need to follow. We cannot register students unless they are in the geographical area of the school. That was a good regulation from the SEC to control the admission process. Before we struggled with admissions. Now the situation is better. But parents are not happy. They are upset if they can't find a place for their daughter and then they complain about us to the newspaper. (Kawla, personal communication, December 20, 2011)

Teachers felt that getting more experience would not reduce the workload due to constant change. Although Lwloa believed that they did not have a heavy workload, she agreed that the constant change affected the school:

> The reason behind the constant change we have is that the people at the SEC are changing. When a new person comes in, he or she doesn't continue with the previous plan, and instead starts from the beginning. This has affected us negatively. Also, the SEC works totally separately from the Evaluation Institute, so sometimes we have to duplicate the work. (Lwloa, personal communication, December 26, 2011)

Rasha agreed that constant change was a challenge in dealing with the SEC:

> For the last seven years, we have had changes every year. Every year I say to myself this year will be more stable and fewer changes will happen. But it's the opposite: we still have constant changes. And the most difficult thing is that these changes happen suddenly and at the wrong time. For example, at the end of the last academic year, as preparation for this year, we did our yearly plan based on our books and the resources that we had. This year the SEC suggested a new yearly plan that does not coincide with our students' books. We made a new booklet for students but I doubt that they will keep it the same next year. (Rasha, personal communication, December 18, 2011)

The school had tried to reduce teachers' workload, but Rasha explained:

> The principal tried to reduce our workload. For example, we didn't participate in the preparation for the national day. And that was good and reduced some of our workload. But now I have the talented student policy that I'm responsible for, and I haven't had time to work on it yet. (Rasha, personal communication, December 18, 2011)

Constant change contributes to workload issues in this school. Rasha elaborated: "The SEC changed the timing of the external workshops from afternoon or evening and they made them during normal working hours from 10:00 until 1:00 and this is good for us." Despite the school's attempts to reduce the workload, most of the teachers I spoke with took work home. Samia said: "My work does not finish at 2:00, I continue working at home. We have lots of paperwork that we have to finish." Dona, a math teacher, described a similar situation: "I work after school until late, sometimes until 1:00 a.m." Fatma faced the same problem, telling me, "I'm a new teacher. The load is too much, and the school requests many things. My husband adds pressure on me. He does not want me to work here because I always take work home." Rasha recognized the same challenge: "Most of the time I take work home to finish it. Sometimes I work [on] weekends and I have been forced to put more pressure on my teachers too, so we can finish the work. This isn't to our advantage and sometimes it has a negative impact on us. I mean pressure and stress kill our motivation." Reham also confirmed that they had a heavy workload. She said: "I had surgery on my back. I'm supposed to leave the school early at 12:00 every day, so I can have some rest. But to be honest, until now I haven't been able to do that, because I have lots of work I have to finish."

Variations in response to workload

As seen in the other two schools, participant perceptions of the workload were varied. The school is required to send the student and staff statistics to the SEC every day before 10:00 a.m. Noura, the student coordinator responsible for filling in the forms, sees it as a time-consuming task. Noura's point was that there was no benefit to doing this task, which she believed increased her workload. Kawla reported: "What is the point of sending students' numbers every single day? We can do it once a month, but I'm not sure what the SEC is doing with all these forms." However, Lwloa thought that filling in the forms was not too difficult. She said, "We are already doing it. We take the absences every day for the school, so we just need to scan the form and send it to the SEC."

Nevertheless, some teachers in this school did not feel their workload to be excessive. For example, Amani, the new science teacher, stated: "It is not a heavy workload. I see it as an opportunity to learn more." From the December observation record on the teachers' room wall chart, it was apparent that Amani had observed other teachers' classes six times. When I talked with her about it, she said, "I'm new and I want to learn from the teachers' experience. Last month, I attended 12 lessons in one month." Amani believed that learning from others was important for her professional growth. Although it required her to do extra work, she perceived it as a valuable aspect of her professional development. Lwloa also believed that the workload was not heavy, commenting as follows on involving teachers in different activities: "These activities are not a load for the staff. They distribute tasks among themselves and they have the yearly calendar where they choose and list the activities. These activities give the teachers a breathing space from routine."

Teachers' and leaders' perceptions of workload can affect their attitudes towards change. I was in the teachers' room and I observed the following discussion between one English teacher and two math teachers about an internal workshop:

> Samia: What is the topic of today's workshop?
>
> Neven: I don't know, I won't be in the school. I have the curriculum workshop at the SEC.
>
> Samia: Lucky you! You won't have to attend the workshop.
>
> Lamia: It's something about IT. It is not very riveting, the important thing is to attend and that's it. I don't think we will hear anything valuable. (Field note, December, 18, 2011)

Amani, in contrast, did not think that classroom observations were a heavy feature of the workload; the teachers in this conversation did not believe that the workshops would be valuable for them. They felt that they needed to attend them because attendance could affect their evaluation. This caused stress for the teachers. During the workshop, Reham was feeling unwell and asked to leave. The principal said: "It's fine with me, but it will affect your evaluation." The principal explained that in some cases the school was forced to follow specific rules. Kawla said: "Sometimes I'm forced to follow regulations from the SEC. For example, teachers' absences affect their evaluation, because the SEC is trying to control teacher absences and to control teachers leaving the school during working hours." Participants' personal lives could affect their work, which could in turn provoke negative emotions in their response to the reform. I observed Rafeea, an English teacher who was tired and complaining about her work. She had been absent the previous day, and said to another teacher: "I came to give my lessons and leave. I have high blood pressure, but I have to come to finish my classes". Hence it is evident that the school faced internal problems with workload, but they also faced external factors from the SEC and parents.

Pressure from parents and the SEC

Observation of this school included the chance to attend a parent-teacher meeting, where I observed interactions between mothers and teachers. Most of the mothers at the meeting were pleased with the school. "There are great teachers who worked hard in this school," said one mother who appreciated her daughter's luck in attending this school rather than her previous one. She added, "My daughter is happy now and so am I." The English teacher, Rafeea, interacted positively with the students' mothers and gave them feedback in a professional way. One mother was really pleased with her daughter's performance in comparison with her previous school. In contrast, Raesa had difficulties with one mother, and in her interview with me about her experience with parents in this school, she explained: "Some parents are supportive but most of them are not. The new system has given them the right to be decision-makers more than is necessary."

Mothers' visits to the classroom were part of the school's various ways of communicating with parents, so that parents could see the school in action. Nuzhat was confident, although slightly nervous. Sarah, the science coordinator, said to her: "You can do it, I'm sure you will be fine". After her lesson, she came to the teachers' room and indicated that she was very pleased, and proud of herself. Nuzhat said:

> I have never had mothers in my class. I'm used to my colleagues who attend and observe my lessons but this is the first time I have had mothers. I was worried and my heart was pounding. I found the girls were nicely behaved, and that was good. The mothers sat quietly at the back of the classroom, and because they had rules to follow, they were cooperative. They were part of my lesson. When I distributed worksheets to my students I also gave them to the mothers. They also participated in the science activities, because I tried to involve them and show them what and how we teach. At the beginning I was worried about what I would do in front of them. After a few minutes I felt they were part of my lesson and their presence seemed normal. (Nuzhat, personal communication, December 26, 2011)

After her lesson, Nuzhat said, "I can relax now; I'm free now until the sixth lesson."

The school was participating in the nationwide scientific research program for schools. Sarah, the science coordinator, was responsible for this program. The SEC gave a limited amount of time to finish their preparation for it. Sarah attended a scientific program meeting at the SEC and the next day met with all the departments to provide information. The school had already started its preparation and the SEC gave them instructions on how to choose a good topic. It was too late, but Sarah explained, "We have to think positively. I understand we are all under pressure and we have to submit this within two weeks." Another teacher commented, "We are always under pressure." It was clear from their questions to Sarah that they did not understand the idea properly or that they needed more clarification. Sarah tried to help her team to cope with their difficulties. In addition to short notice, communication with the SEC was another challenge for the school. Noura said:

> It's difficult to deal with the SEC. Sometimes they request things that sap our energies. They send a message or an email telling us to attend a workshop or a training session on the same day that the message is sent. We need to know about this in advance. Then they ask us to implement what we have learned from the training within a limited time. For example, they asked us to update the students' and also staff information on the system, but they gave us only a week to finish this task. This is impossible. And sometimes they ask us to do something which is not clear to us because they are not clear about it themselves. (Noura, personal communication, December 26, 2011)

To implement change, leaders need time, clarity about new policies, and the opportunity to implement a few changes at a time. The principal, Kawla, reported three main difficulties with the SEC:

> The main challenge for me is working with the SEC. The timing of new policies is not right because they send new ones when we already have our own system and when it's also the middle of term. Secondly, unclear policies need clear instructions. Finally, we don't have the freedom or flexibility we need to implement their program. (Kawla, personal communication, December 20, 2011)

Raesa also faced challenges with the SEC because of her new responsibility as a subject coordinator:

> Nothing satisfies the curriculum office. They are asking us to do different tasks every few months and most of these requests are unclear to us. For example, last year when I started teaching in the foundation stage, they asked us to implement circle time [1] as a teaching strategy. The Early Years specialist from the SEC came only an hour to explain

---

(1) Circle time is an activity in which students and their teacher sit together to develop pupils' speaking and listening skills. It is about discussion, reflection, emotional understanding and making connections. The whole process enhances the self-esteem of students both academically and socially.

what we were supposed to do. It was not clear to me at all. We needed someone to explain it fully and show us how to implement the strategy. They asked us to integrate three subjects together, but this was hard for me. (Raesa, personal communication, December 25, 2011)

In sum, the senior management worked well together. Kawla and Lwloa were close, having been friends and colleagues for most of their professional lives. Thus, they understood and supported each other. Their leadership style was transferred into the English and science departments, which managed the reform requirements very well. However, the math and Arabic departments struggled with collaboration and staff shortages, and other leaders in the school needed to support them. The school faced workload challenges, although staff did not uniformly express them as onerous. Rather, some staff viewed the reform's new requirements as important for their professional growth. Constant change in school policies and communication with the SEC were the main difficulties experienced by the leaders.

Chapter Seven

EMPOWERING LEADER CONFRONTING DISRUPTIVE STUDENT BEHAVIOR

Gulf School

It was the beginning of January. Gulf School was stunned and saddened by the news of a school trip accident in another school, which had left a girl in intensive care for over three days. Despite this incident, Fahad, the vice-principal for administration, was very confident about student safety in his school: "We have clear policies about student trips, but accidents could happen inside or outside the school." However, he admitted there were problems with student behavior:

> The MoE was a good system of controlling student behavior, but it lacked a quality curriculum. I do not agree with physical punishment—this was phased out as long ago as the 1980s. Now we have to understand students at this age. Teachers need to control themselves and use ways that won't harm students in dealing with student behavior. (Fahad, personal communication, January 8, 2012)

The school was established in 2004 with most of its staff working there for more than six years. The school is located in the capital, Doha, and has around 700 students in Grades 7–9 (12- to 14-year-olds). It has some 50 teachers and 20 administrators.

In the first meeting, Fahad gave some instructions to me as a female researcher in a boys' school. He said: "During the five minutes between classes, when students move from one class to another, I would prefer you not to be around. I am worried that some students might say something inappropriate to you." As a result, he gave me the school timetable, so I was aware of the times between classes. However, his colleague Omar disagreed with him: "I don't think that will be a problem, we always have female consultants or visitors from the SEC." Subsequently, Fahad asked me if I would need an escort while I was walking around and I said this would not be necessary.

From my observations, especially during breaks and the time between lessons, I found teachers were struggling to manage student behavior. I witnessed a lack of respect in how students talk to their teachers. Although this was a concern for the leaders, it was important for me to observe teacher and leader interaction with students and to explain to Fahad how that observation would be valuable for me.

Omar sent a message to the subject coordinators requesting a quick meeting. I gave a brief summary about my research and they clarified my research purpose by asking more details. After the meeting, Omar walked me around the building and introduced me to the rest of the staff. From the first day, the school environment seemed calm and clean, with the open spaces and bright lights of a modern school. On the second floor, a group of teachers talked loudly as they walked towards the meeting room. They were curious about my reasons for being there, and, when approached, they were eager to tell their stories.

I did not feel comfortable at the beginning as all eyes were on me, because of my style of dress, wearing a traditional dress (abaya)[1] that distinguished me as a Qatari woman. After spending time familiarizing both them and me with this new situation, I began to feel more comfortable as a female researcher in a boys' school context. Conducting my study in a boys' school disproved

---

(1) An abaya is a voluminous black over-garment used by women across the Arabian Gulf region. It is worn with a shayla (headscarf) and provides a strong visual indicator in this context of the researcher's gender and nationality. Since non-segregated professional environments in Qatar are relatively recent (and the response to a visibly foreign female researcher unlikely to be similar) a certain degree of initial uncertainty was perceived from both myself as a researcher and the boys' school as to how appropriately to navigate the situation. The initial caution due to innate cultural protective instincts towards females was quickly resolved, and the eventual openness and receptivity from the boys' school was such that the data obtained was of more than satisfactory quality.

my expectations of the difficulties of a female researcher in such a context. I had expected some resistance, but I found none. Also, I was able to observe the staff as though I were not there, which was very helpful for my data collection. Their interactions with each other were natural. For example, I spent time in the teachers' room and talk flowed easily among the teachers. They were comfortable with each other and did not seem to mind me in their midst.

The school faces several internal challenges, including disruptive student behavior, staff resistance to change, and unnecessary paperwork. They also face difficulties in implementing external policies such as the Information and Communication Technology (ICT) policy from the SEC. Each of these difficulties is described in the following subsections.

Saeed, the principal, is a very tall man in his late thirties, a soft-spoken and thoughtful leader who was eager to show me the best of his school. Many told me of the autonomy that Saeed's leadership permits. One English teacher noted: "I have friends in other schools and I know authoritarian principals who give orders and tell everyone what to do, but Mr. Saeed does not do that." Another teacher described Mr. Saeed as: "… wonderful; I have stayed at this school because of our leader." Saeed strives to create a school which increases the sense of community or family (a word he often uses) and which dismantles the hierarchical arrangements of prescribed social roles. I was shadowing Anwar, but Saeed sent the receptionist to ask me to attend the award-giving ceremony for the admin staff, reflecting: "You might be thinking that we do this for show, but I know our staff want to stay here because we always appreciate their efforts."

Student behavior: then and now

Speaking openly about the situation, the leaders reported a lack of control over the boys in this age group. They confirmed that the SEC policy did not help them to manage student behavior. The interviewee felt that student behavior affected student academic performance and well-being, also affecting teachers' classroom management abilities and their relationships with students. The participants differed in their views about managing student behavior.

Two years before my visit, some serious problems had occurred. When there were fights or problems with teachers, although parents were brought in immediately, they often felt problems were not solved adequately and they used to complain formally at the police station. Two years ago a new solution was introduced. Since the school gave the teachers' mobile phone numbers to parents, there have been no misunderstandings because parents communicate directly, thus ending the need for police station visits. Saeed sympathetically remarked, "It was not easy for me to solve fight problems in the police station."

I witnessed that parents could call and come at any time during the school day. For example, during Anwar's interview he received a call from a mother asking about the math units that would be included in the test. Also, a father came to the principal's office during my interview to meet with him without prior appointment. The father entered the principal's office to discuss some issues about his son and to thank the school for their support. Dealing with parents used to pose a major challenge, but the principal and the vice-principal agreed that they had now established the best way to communicate with parents. Saeed said:

> Before, we had problems with parents, but now we have fewer misunderstandings. We gave parents the staff's mobile numbers, so they can communicate with teachers and coordinators directly. We also communicate with parents in different ways such as in parents' meetings and newsletters. In addition to these points of contact, parents can observe classes and attend office hours. (Saeed, personal communication, January 9, 2012)

I asked Fahad about the communication between parents and staff. He commented:

> I think this solution [giving parents the staff's mobile numbers] has more advantages than disadvantages. It is better that there is more communication between the school and parents, because not all parents can come to the school; most of them are busy. The one significant disadvantage is that parents can call teachers during the weekend or at evening time, and this annoys teachers. (Fahad, personal communication, January 8, 2012)

Ahmed, the English coordinator, worked as an English teacher for two years in the MoE schools, then joined the independent school when it was established in 2004 as a head of department. A man in his thirties, he has energy that keeps him on the move. He reflected:

> We are tools to implement the SEC policies. From our experience we found many problems with the behavior policy. We are struggling with the boys at this level and the policy did not help us to manage student behavior. We have to be careful with the SEC, because if the school has problems with the student behavior then the SEC will be very strict about it because this will upset them. We try to solve bad student behavior internally and avoid involving the SEC. (Ahmed, personal communication, January 12, 2012)

Omar, the vice-principal for academic studies, is a very large man with broad shoulders in his late fifties. He has had 30 years' experience in education and plans to retire in a year's time. Everyone praises Omar; their respect for him springs from their long association with him, from his commitment to the school, and from his outspoken defence of his teachers. Omar also agreed that the behavior policy was not helpful for the school because they were not given any authority and parents have the full right to complain. He pointed out:

> This [the preparatory level] is a difficult stage, which is different from the primary and secondary levels. Students' psychology and physiology are changing throughout this

stage. The behavior policy is not helpful, because it sometimes makes the situation worse. Students don't care because they think the teachers have no power. Most of the time teachers get frustrated about student misbehavior because it affects their lessons and their teaching methods. (Omar, personal communication, January 10, 2012)

Abdulkareem, an English teacher with 18 years' teaching experience, agreed, explaining that under the new system the focus is on the curriculum and not on behavior, saying:

We have loads of information and the level of the curriculum is very high for students. The focus is on the curriculum but there is no focus on student behavior policies, especially here in the boys' schools. On the other hand, in the MoE there was a lack of quality curricula, but there was more focus on classroom management and schools had more control over student behavior. (Abdulkareem, personal communication, January 10, 2012)

Student misbehavior: the unpleasant consequences

Overcrowding is a problem. The new schools planned by the SEC are not yet finished, so schools currently implementing the reform must accept more students than they are equipped for. Behavior is often affected. Mahmoude, a science teacher, wanted to add variety to his lessons by having students do more investigations, but he felt that classroom management and student behavior constrained that desire. He said:

I believe in the importance of using a variety of strategies in teaching science, especially scientific enquiry. But my problem is dealing with a large number of students, most of whom don't care about learning and about school in general. Sometimes, I go to my lesson with excitement, but it ends with disappointment because I have spent most of my time dealing with their behavior. (Mahmoude, personal communication, January 1, 2012)

Mahmoude believed that student attitudes to learning affected his teaching strategies. With 30–32 students in each classroom, he felt more pressure to focus on their behavior rather than teaching scientific concepts. Imad also had the same difficulties with student numbers: "Before we had 18 students in each classroom but now we have 30. This affects our work badly." Suffian agreed that student numbers are a challenge for them:

> We have become like the MoE again, with more than 30 students in each classroom. This affects teaching and learning; this is too large a number to do activities in the science lab. Groups are big, so not all students will have the opportunity to participate. For example, I teach measuring voltage; I have a limited number of voltmeters, so not all students can take part in this. (Suffian, personal communication, January 11, 2012)

Furthermore, Khaled, a science teacher, clarified that this overcrowding has a negative impact on their performance as teachers. He remarked, "we are blamed if we do not develop our skills or if we can't manage students' behavior and this affects our position in the school."

Anwar, the math coordinator, is an experienced leader who manages his team effectively. When he begins to talk about things that are important to him, energy and enthusiasm light his intense eyes. He is well respected by his colleagues. He said: "I have always found that the more power I give my teachers, the more responsibility they take." Anwar expressed another view, namely that student behavior is the school's responsibility:

> Supervising students during breaks is an extra load for teachers. The SEC sent a circular advising schools not to involve teachers in these duties because they are already busy. We don't have enough supervisors so the school delegated this task throughout all the staff. My team resisted this task, but I think we can spend time with students doing activities that we couldn't do during our normal lessons. We have

difficulties with student behavior, so we need to be close to them outside the classroom. It is our responsibility to understand students and we can do this during break time. (Anwar, personal communication, January 9, 2012)

Managing student behavior

Both Anwar and Suffian believed that the school, even outside class time, can contribute significantly to adequate student behavior management. Anwar was positive; even though he disagreed with involving teachers in supervising students at break time, he tried to find a way to convince his team to use break time to solve behavior issues. Break time was a particular problem because teachers believed that supervising students was the administration's responsibility. Anwar blamed the school for bad student behavior and believed that the school had the responsibility to monitor students and to try to come up with solutions. Suffian emphasized the critical nature of the teenage years: "Adolescence is a difficult stage. We have to understand students because this can affect their performance and as a result, it will affect the outcome of the new reform." These reflections offered by Gulf School staff demonstrated a willingness to offer solutions to an aspect of school life—student behavior—that they perceive as a part of their professional responsibility.

Mohammed, the Arabic coordinator, is a middle-aged man with a PhD in Arabic. He came to Gulf School in 2004. After three years, he became the coordinator. He explained the relationship he saw between student academic performance and psychology, and the importance of teacher training on this relationship. He added that to manage this critical issue, parents, students and the school needed to work together.

> If we want to improve student academic performance, we have to focus on student psychology and emotional character. In this matter we can't work alone; we need support from parents, who have an important role in shaping student

behavior. We also need support from the school management and the student himself. All these elements are important in managing student behavior. I don't believe that shouting and beating students are the right strategies. (Mohammed, personal communication, January 8, 2012)

Mohammed, the Arabic coordinator, agreed with Suffian on the importance of understanding students at this age, offering:

We need people who are qualified in understanding boys of this age. This is important. When we have a misbehaving student, the solution is not to shout at him or call his father, or make him write a pledge. Instead we have to listen to the student first. The problem is that teachers lack understanding of the psychology of this age, therefore they need more training on this important issue. (Mohammed, personal communication, January 8, 2012)

Omar believed that training was not always the solution to the problem of developing teacher practices, because, as he said:

The problem is that some teachers cannot improve how they deal with problem students. If a teacher doesn't have the natural ability, training won't work and won't help him to handle the problem. (Omar, personal communication, January 10, 2012)

I was curious about the student behavior policy, so I spent time studying it in order to discern the reasons for participants' complaints. The policy is available on the SEC website. It seemed to me like any other policy that can be found in any school. The next day, I tried to discover more and to understand the problem. I found that the real complaint was not about the actual policy but about the difficulty of dealing with problems at the class level. So, when a teacher had a problem with a student, the student was sent to the social worker, and the teacher felt powerless.

The above leaders expressed their views about the importance of understanding student psychology in order to manage student behavior. These opinions contrast sharply with those of Arabic teacher Yousef, who kept a long and thick stick in the teachers' room and took it with him in his lessons to intimidate students. He said:

> I would prefer to go back to the MoE when we had more control over student behavior. I have more than 20 years' experience and I used to use this stick and I had more respect from my students. Now I just use it to intimidate my students. The new behavior policy won't allow us to use such punishment. (Yousef, personal communication, January 11, 2012)

Yousef was proud of his way of controlling his students and using physical punishment as a way to get their respect. He recognized the general difficulties in his class and spoke of it as a "hard class to teach." He believed his problems stemmed from the wide variation of academic abilities and the lack of effectiveness of behavior policy. Saeed set out his approach to student punishment:

> I don't allow teachers to exclude students from their lessons. This affects student learning. This is still happening in the school, because some teachers lose control. I am trying to encourage teachers to solve problems of bad behavior without excluding students. (Saeed, personal communication, January 9, 2012)

Positive views about the reform

Despite student behavior problems, all participants had positive views about the reform. Their individual objectives related not to the reform as a whole but rather to some parts of the reform. They were concerned about the negative aspects of the reform for learners and teachers. On the first day, I met Fahad, the vice-principal for administration, and Omar, the vice-principal for academic studies. Fahad, before coming to Gulf School, had been a school-based social worker, and although many of his skills in working with students must have been transferable to the new environment, a certain degree of surprise may have overshadowed his experience in moving from the MoE system to an independent school setting. He remarked: "The work here is different from the MoE system; although I was mainly dealing with students and their problems, the whole system was boring. To work in the new system of course we need to improve our skills, and by working here, I feel my skills have grown dramatically." I asked him to be specific about the new skills he has acquired. He offered, "Working as a team and dealing with parents. Parents now are different and we have to be careful," adding, "Before joining Gulf School, I had heard rumors that independent schools are chaos, but when I joined, I discovered just the opposite."

In contrast, Fahad's opinion differed in relation to the reform, in particular the speed of implementation:

> The idea of the reform and the reasons behind it are important. However, the problem is with the speed of implementation and the unclear plan at the beginning of the reform, especially in the first three years. Now, things are getting more organized. Now, we have tests and behavior policies in place, lessons and the curriculum are the same for all the schools. Before, it was controlled by each school with its own rules and procedures. (Fahad, personal communication, January 8, 2012)

Although Ahmed and Fahad had a positive attitude towards the educational reform, they both mentioned some difficulties such as the increase in student numbers and the speed of implementation. They had contrasting ideas regarding the progress of the reform. Fahad believed that at the beginning of the implementation there were few centralized education policies. Now, each school has fallen into line with a centrally directed policy.

Ahmed, the English coordinator, has a positive view about the educational reform, stating:

> The idea of the educational reform is excellent. At the beginning it was more successful, but now the situation is difficult

and getting worse. For example, before we had 20 students in each classroom, but now we have 30 and sometimes 32 students. This is a big challenge for us. We used to use technology and group work more easily than now. Now when I have three students who have difficulties with their laptops during my lesson, I am distracted and my lesson time is wasted, because I have to deal with technology problems; classroom management also will be an issue. (Ahmed, personal communication, January 12, 2012)

Abdulkareem believed that the reform had a positive impact on the learners in improving their use of the English language. He said:

I look at my lessons 10 years ago versus the ones I'm currently teaching; there's no comparison. We used to teach students the English alphabet from Grade 5 at the age of 11. And in each term students learned maximum 20–25 words. Now under the new system, students start learning the language from pre-school, that is, from the age of three. We used to teach for the test, but students now can talk, discuss and write in English. (Abdulkareem, personal communication, January 10, 2012)

Suffian, the science coordinator, also commented on the way student learners benefited from the reform. A thin, nervous person, he had teaching experience inside and outside Qatar. When the science meeting was over, I approached him and asked about his general idea of the reform. He leaned in close to talk to me, but nervously checked his colleagues for validation. His hands were always moving, either fiddling with his folders or twisting his fingers. Suffian commented: "I am with the reform; it is a great initiative because it focuses on active learning and the use of technology. This is totally different from 20 years ago, when passive learning was commonplace."

Ahmed added that the reform had a benefit for the teachers as well. However, to Ahmed, "decision-making" has a more limited meaning, signifying only the identification of the way for him and his team to implement the new policy:

> The new reform allowed enough room for teachers and coordinators to take decisions. Even though we received instructions to implement policies from the SEC, still we have freedom on the way to implement policies. My role as a coordinator is that I try to find a way to make life easier for my teachers. (Ahmed, personal communication, January 12, 2012)

When I asked Anwar about his view of the reform, he stated his belief that the reform was beneficial for the learners and for him as a teacher. He learns at the same time as his students, which implies attentive work on his part to keep up. He observed:

> The reform is an excellent initiative. Before we used to teach using traditional ways, where the learner was passive. I don't mean the whole of the MoE system was wrong, but it was necessary to develop our way of teaching students in line with the 21st–century requirement. Teaching under the reform [as opposed to prior to the reform] makes learning more relevant to the students, providing valuable knowledge and skills. I learn something new every year from teaching these students. (Anwar, personal communication, January 9, 2012)

Saeed's idea of the reform was not similar to the others: "Under the reform, we have seen improvements in many different aspects, such as student learning, teacher training, teaching resources and new teaching strategies. However, it is too early to judge the result of the reform. We are still experimenting and each time we learn from our mistakes." Saeed added caution to this statement:

> We need appropriate and accurate planning. The problem is that, when we face a difficulty, then the SEC's action was to change the policy. Why do we wait until problems happen before we improve our strategies? We need to avoid mistakes before they happen. For example, at the beginning of the

reform, specialization in education was not a requirement for the school principal. After many problems, they changed that policy. It should be an important requirement from the beginning. (Saeed, personal communication, January 9, 2012)

Omar, the vice-principal for academic studies, said:

> Qatar has invested a lot in reforming the education system. The idea of the reform is excellent [but] we can't judge the outcomes yet—it is too early to do so. But I am optimistic. It is a reform of the whole system, including the curriculum, teaching methods, finance, recruitment, resources and other. We can't say that all of it has been implemented to the same standard. Most of the ideas that come from the SEC are good but the instructions are not clear. For example, with the student elections and the scientific research program, the objectives are great but the implementation was not good. The reform now needs to be revised. Many mistakes have been made. (Omar, personal communication, January 10, 2012)

Implementation difficulties: ever-increasing paperwork

Although the reform has benefits for the learner, it also has undeniable difficulties such as curriculum content and time pressure for school instructors and leaders. Ali, an English teacher, said:

> We teach students a load of information. This is a major burden for student as well as teacher. Grade 7 students are being taught at what used to be a secondary level. Such a change needs to be implemented gradually. To gain the benefit of the reform, change needs sufficient time so we can get the best result. (Ali, personal communication, January 12, 2012)

Student behavior was not the only problem they faced. Most interviewees have problems with paperwork and documentation. Saeed stated: "The problem is that people who make decisions are far away from the reality and are not fully aware of what is going on inside schools." Similarly, Anwar described the same challenge with documentation:

> Most of our documentation is for show only. Some coordinators compete to see who has more folders; some have 20 and others have 25 folders. We have to document everything. So, when the SEC or the EI come they check our work. Some of this documentation does not reflect our real work. (Anwar, personal communication, January 9, 2012)

Ahmed had the same view:

> The major challenge for me is too much paperwork and too little time, that is why most of our teachers take work home. Sometimes I have to follow up with my team by phoning during the weekend or in the evening while I am with my family. Sometimes we have to come to school in the evening if there is something urgent. (Ahmed, personal communication, January 12, 2012)

Teachers believe this paperwork to be an inappropriate indicator of teacher effort and attainment. Rather, in their view, a focus on such documents risks under-representing or, at times, unrealistically inflating the levels of professional input, while merely adding to an already demanding workload. Ahmed said: "Records are helpful, but sometimes it is not an accurate description of our procedures. We can write something that we did not achieve or it could be the opposite: we could do something important without writing about it." The reason for excessive paperwork was the yearly changing lesson plans, which posed a challenge for some departments, as Anwar's comments show:

> The constant changes in lesson plans have increased our stress and affected our work negatively. The lesson plans are always changing. These changes are affecting the students and parents as well. (Anwar, personal communication, January 9, 2012)

However, Ahmed believed that the content of lesson plans had not changed but that the format had, and affirmed:

> I don't have this problem (changes in lesson plans); I used to have it at the beginning of the reform. Maybe a new teacher will complain about it. Now most of my teachers have at least six years' experience working under the reform, because they have already gone through the process. (Ahmed, personal communication, January 12, 2012)

Artificial workloads

Saeed signalled an important issue about workload. Documentation had caused heavy workload, or as Saeed called it, "artificial loads," commenting:

> We have "artificial loads". By this I mean that some leaders ask their team to do unnecessary tasks because they want to show that they are the boss. This adds a great burden to teachers. I am not saying we don't have a heavy workload, but coordinators can play a role in creating more and more work. (Saeed, personal communication, January 9, 2012)

Saeed's explanation demonstrates that although teachers had fifteen hours teaching per week (which is not a big load for them compared with teacher timetables in other countries), they still feel overloaded by superficial bureaucratic tasks. Omar offered solutions to minimize workload:

> I agree we have a heavy workload, especially the teachers. However, I believe that workload is not an issue for teachers who have been working for more than three years. Being more accustomed to the workload, the more experienced teachers can do their work in a shorter period of time. Also working in a team could alleviate this issue. I agree staff have more work when they have to finish many tasks at the same time. My role is to reduce these loads and to not ask for many things at the same time. (Omar, personal communication, January 10, 2012)

Training and professional development: growing difficulties

Teacher training presented another major challenge. These difficulties indicate its complexities and importance. Professional development and training could help in implementing reform requirements such as improving teaching skills and knowledge. Anwar had difficulties in teaching some math skills such as critical thinking and problem-solving under the reform, giving the reasons behind these difficulties:

> The reform focuses on new teaching and learning approaches such as reasoning, problem-solving and critical thinking. The difficulties are in implementing these strategies. Firstly, some teachers didn't believe in these new methods, preferring to teach what they used to. Secondly, some teachers don't have the sufficient skills and knowledge to teach problem-solving and critical thinking. For example, data-handling requires interpreting abstract numbers and linking these to student life practices, but some teachers find this difficult. (Anwar, personal communication, January 9, 2012)

However, training is often not a complete solution to the challenge of changing attitudes (and consequently behavior patterns) towards the reform. Omar could discern the value of certain forms of training:

> When I was working in the MoE, I thought that a good teacher was one who would have strong knowledge of the subject primarily, but now after my experience under the reform, I have realized that a good teacher needs a variety of teaching methods and the ability to use a variety of technological methods. This change in attitude came after lots of training and workshops. (Omar, personal communication, January 10, 2012)

Saeed stated that the quality of training was more important than the number of hours spent attending professional development that was often not beneficial for staff:

I am against any training that adds to teacher workloads. If the teacher has training on a weekly basis, how will he implement what he had learned in his lessons? Focus should be on the quality of the PD (professional development), not the quantity. In some schools they compete about how many hours teachers spend on the training. (Saeed, personal communication, January 9, 2012)

Resistance to change: a core leadership challenge

Leaders have to deal with resistance as part of the change. Ahmed said, "Sometimes I face some resistance from one or two teachers; I am not obliged to push the policy through, but I convince them of its worth by showing the positive side of the new policy. The result is that most of the time they join us." Anwar sees three categories of possible resisters. The first group he called "ordinary teachers". By normal teachers, Anwar was referring to "the group that is satisfied with their way of teaching. They like the MoE system, and their lesson plans have not changed for more than 10 years. They copy and paste without changes …they are not innovators." The second group he called "resisters to change." He defined this group as "those who refuse change most of the time and resist. Sometimes they affect others negatively." The third group contained those "who don't know their position—one day they accept change and another day they resist. In my role as a leader I have to understand each group and try to find a way to convince them to accept the change. I work mostly with the third group, because with encouragement they come along with the team."

Some of the changes seemed difficult but one of the important roles fulfilled by the leaders was illustrating the value of the change to those who resisted it. Ahmed explained his way of dealing with such teachers, commenting:

I have a group that resists change and they don't want to participate in implementing the new policy. I use it with the group who accept and don't have difficulties. Then I try to

> show the resistant group the benefit of the new methods. I always try to implement policy with them and most of the time they fall into line with the rest of the team. (Ahmed, personal communication, January 12, 2012)

Omar believed that his school did not include resisters; rather, he referred to "less motivated staff," saying:

> We don't have teachers who resist change, because everyone knows that they don't have options: they have to follow these rules. I try to build teams that can support each other. I always make sure to have a combination of motivated and less motivated teachers, because they encourage each other. But I have to be careful about the latter group, which can have a bad influence. (Omar, personal communication, January 10, 2012)

Challenges from the outside: ICT implementation

During my first school tour, I stopped by a large, dark room; the door had a glass window, showing the room's interior. Mr. Ahmed asked for the key from the IT manager; inside, the room was dark, cold and covered with dust. Almost brand-new computers and piles of equipment lay on the floor. The school participated in two major technological projects, both implemented by ictQatar: the e-Schoolbag and Knowledge Net, a learning management system. The e-Schoolbag started in 2007, and it was implemented in four schools, Gulf School being one of them. All the participants with whom I discussed this problem had previously been very enthusiastic about the projects, and greatly regretted their sudden discontinuation. However, they felt powerless to change the situation and were ultimately resigned to the situation. The SEC's sudden discontinuation of these ICT projects is indicative of the general climate of constant unpredictable change. Saeed described the beginning of the initiative as one that "…was a huge project and it cost a lot, especially in teacher training and in the infrastructure. They trained teachers to use it in their teaching. It was used in the main four subjects." Imad, the English teacher who participated heavily in these two projects, described their end:

> We started many ICT projects but we stopped. The e-Schoolbag and Knowledge Net were the major ones. We worked on these two projects for a long time. We did training for almost two years, three hours per week. We accomplished a lot. We constructed a website for teaching resources based on our curriculum for all of the schools. Teachers did intensive training and suddenly this project disappeared. There was no long-term plan. (Imad, personal communication, January 9, 2012)

Ahmed, the English coordinator, talked about the implementation of the projects:

> I used the e-bag in my teaching and it was useful. Later we found that the resources in some subjects were not well integrated with our curriculum, so the SEC changed the company that was charged with designing the software's integration with the existing curriculum. Then teachers started training again; every time we started they changed something, then we started training again; and all of this was too much. I think it became like a commercial business for these companies who found a good source of profit in this upheaval. (Ahmed, personal communication, January 12, 2012)

According to Mohammed, ICT projects manager, there were four reasons behind the failure of the projects:

> There was conflict between ictQatar and the SEC in leading the project. Secondly, there were technical problems, because no one was responsible for the project inside the school. Therefore, we were overloaded. We were volunteers but we had other tasks to do. Thirdly, there wasn't a long-term and clear plan for the project. We had general objectives, but there was no detail or timeline. The professional development was good but it could have been better.

> It could have provided lessons for teachers to learn. Finally, a funding deficit affected the continuation of the project. (Mohammed, personal communication, January 10, 2012)

Saeed was sad about the failure of the ICT project and suggested different reasons for it:

> They implemented these projects very quickly without doing enough research. During the implementation, problems arose which they had not anticipated and they did not know how to solve them. In addition, these two projects were implemented in other countries; the trouble was that they introduced them here without filtering out culturally unsuitable topics. Another reason was that when these projects came under the IT office at the SEC, it became more difficult because we were dealing with technicians rather than education specialists. (Saeed, personal communication, Janaury 9, 2012)

Decision-making and collaboration

Although the school faced challenges in reform implementation, most of the departments worked well together. During my observations of the English department's meeting, the English examination was discussed. Teachers found that it was too much for the student to have a long test, so they suggested detaching the writing section. There were several parts of the English exam, and in the meeting they discussed separating the writing part from the rest of the exam. The new change allowed students more time for writing, as this section occurred on a different day from the rest of the examination. All staff members participated in the discussion. Sometimes they disagreed with each other, but in the end they came to a unanimous conclusion. After the meeting I had the opportunity to talk with Ahmed (the coordinator) about involving his team in decision-making. He said:

> I couldn't take this decision by myself; I have to consult with my colleagues. It is a change for them, but my role is

to find a way to implement it and involve my team. This is very important. It wasn't easy to bring heads together but we agreed after a very long discussion. Some disagreed at the beginning, others argued throughout, but in the end we managed to get a kind of agreement. (Ahmed, personal communication, January 12, 2012)

Saeed also agreed with the importance of involving his team in decision-making, stating: "I like to involve my teachers and to talk with them. I prefer this because it will convince them. And they can implement new decisions easier this way." Although the leaders themselves were not really involved in decision-making (which was mandated from the SEC), they tried to include their teams wherever possible.

As a way of collaborating between departments, teachers observed each other's classes and exchanged classroom visits. Ahmed believed that collaboration between departments and sharing ideas would improve teaching, stating: "Last week we had a science teacher who observed an English lesson to learn about classroom management. The principal suggested this exchange visit. Sharing best practices is the best way to improve."

Anwar also understood the value of collaborative work to improve teaching skills, commenting:

> In our department's professional development program, I always encourage internal and external visits between teachers. Sometimes our teachers visit other schools to learn from their practices. I am responsible for arranging this with my colleagues in other schools. In these visits, teachers learn and share their teaching practices. This is so important in teaching math. (Anwar, personal communication, January 9, 2012)

Collaboration also took place in interdepartmental discussions in the hallways between classes. A group of teachers talked together periodically to coordinate their approach to a specific teaching unit and to share successful teaching strategies. For example, the English teachers would converse with the science teachers quickly during the five minutes between classes and break time.

Teachers, with their coordinators, sought out and received help from each other about their pedagogical strategies. They shared ideas, for example, in the math department; they discussed problems using mental methods to add and subtract decimals in simple cases. In science, they discussed the periodic table and energy resources. However, they did not share ideas about why students might be struggling with those same scientific or mathematical concepts. When I talked to some teachers about sharing ideas, none reported how this collaboration would improve their lessons. Instead, what they reported to me was a more general appreciation of this sharing.

A supportive team is an essential component in dealing with change. Ahmed was proud of his team, saying:

> I have been working with my team for more than six years. We are friends more than colleagues; we support each other. And honestly, we are cooperative. I have a very good team. Sometimes we disagree but we work well together. (Ahmed, personal communication, January 12, 12)

Anwar, the math coordinator, had been teaching for over 20 years, and the math department culture bore his influence. He set an example of collaborative working relationships and encouraged collaboration among the teachers. For example, Anwar and his team developed new teaching strategies based on math topics. He made copies available for all the teachers to try. He set a tone of collaborative openness to new ideas. Anwar is a calm leader, and his positive emotional responses were reflected in the way he led his team. He had some teachers who resisted change; he explained to me how he managed teachers in these categories in a manner that avoided their anger and frustration. The leaders' personalities and their responses to change critically affected the way they dealt with it.

Science department: struggle with collaboration

In contrast, I observed a substantial amount of non-collaborative work in the school's science department, with Suffian particularly suffering in this regard. After observing two of their weekly science department meetings, I noticed that Suffian was not comfortable working with his team. He seemed very stressed, highly anxious, and prone to be short-tempered. Suffian felt the lack of a supportive team to help him cope with the change. For example, negative teacher responses to his requests and their poor participation reflected a negative working relationship between the members. He commented:

> I am aware that my team do[es]n't work well together. I always encourage them to share and to learn from each other. For example, I created a folder in which we share science teaching materials. But still I have difficulties with some teachers. Some need more support in strengthening teaching and some need to work better with other teachers. I even have to call one of the teachers to get him to come in every morning. He is not resistant to change, he is just not committed to work. (Suffian, personal communication, January 11, 2012)

Both Anwar and Suffian worked towards building a strong and coherent team. In Anwar's case, however, his team was helping him to achieve this by working collaboratively, whereas Suffian's team members were less motivated and less committed to working together. A good relationship between the team members can help the leaders to manage change, and team members have some responsibility in building the team.

Building a team also requires a good leader, as described by Saeed: "I don't like individual decision-making, I prefer to talk with my team. We discuss together and come up with a single conclusion; this makes implementation much easier." Mohammed, an Arabic teacher, proudly stated:

> I have to understand my team and consider their personal problems. I have to encourage them and support them.

> We have been working together for a long time and we understand each other well. My team doesn't follow my instructions because I am their coordinator, but because we have a good working relationship. (Mohammed, personal communication, January 8, 2012)

This collaboration was clear when I observed how Mohammed dealt with and talked with his team in their weekly meetings, asking for their advice and consulting them.

Ultimately, many staff were satisfied with the autonomy that the principal's leadership office permitted. The principal strives to create a school that increases the sense of community and dismantles the hierarchical arrangement of roles in the school. Suffian, the science coordinator, an experienced leader, but very anxious, faces lack of staff commitment to teamwork, despite his best efforts to motivate them and explain reform requirements. The school faces internal problems, such as disruptive student behavior, teacher resistance to change, and increased paperwork. Staff also complain about ICT projects imposed by the SEC. Student behavior was identified as the main issue. Although the school had tried to solve this problem, some teachers found the result unsatisfactory. In general, teachers felt that parents were given too much power to interfere.

Chapter Eight

GROUP PORTRAIT: CROSS–CASE ANALYSIS AND DISCUSSION

In the preceding four chapters, I have presented a portrait of four schools. Each school operates in particular ways, yet all share common characteristics. In this chapter, I present the differing perceptions of educational reform expressed by the leaders that I portrayed. I consider the four portraits together, including discussions of similarities and differences under five main themes that emerged from the data. The key themes are organized according to four primary research questions, presented in Figure 5.

A number of subthemes are collapsed under the five major themes: workload, collaboration, emotional response to change, conditions for change and leaders' challenge (see Figure 5). By analysing the data, I started with an initial categorization of nine themes. In order to build up a more in-depth picture of each school, its events, environments and idiosyncrasies, the original nine themes were later re-classified into five. It emerged that what appeared to be separate themes were in fact aspects of a broader one. For example, at the outset, 'resistance to change' had been separately classified, but a closer reading of the data revealed that a more appropriate location would have been to place that within 'leader challenges'. Conversely, 'workload' emerged and remained as a separate theme, it being prominent in the data in all four schools.

A close analysis of these themes revealed that the first two research questions addressing ways school leaders interpret school change and its place in ENE along with their roles in managing the reform led to the first four themes. This is described in the first section of this chapter: Leaders' perceptions of the reform and how those leaders are managing the implementation. In the second section, I turn to the third and fourth research question on leaders' challenges by presenting the final theme (See Figure 5).

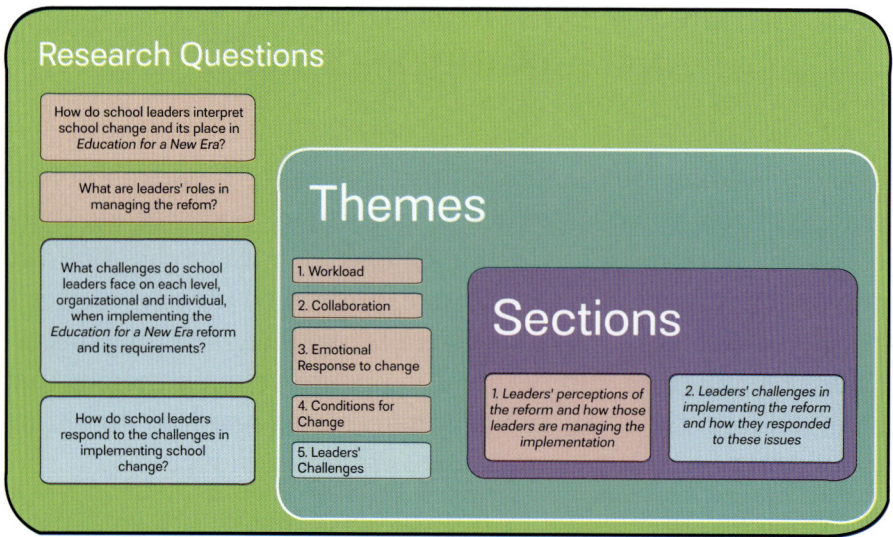

Figure 5. Group portrait glimpse

In this chapter, I draw upon the detailed accounts given by the four main leaders in my formal and informal interviews, observations, and field notes. I present and analyse the practices, views, and beliefs that shaped their behavior whilst managing educational reform by using examples from the portraits and references presented herein. As reported in Figure 6, the four main leaders in this study are the principals of each school:

> Amna is a leader in her late forties with more than 20 years' experience in schools. Described by her assistant as "the engine of the school," she tries to involve her staff in decision-making, but they always go back for her final word. Although a very committed leader who believes in the idea of the reform, she expressed disappointment when she talked about the lack of support from the SEC.
>
> Salwa, a tall confident woman in her late thirties, is a very caring leader who is trying to build a family environment. Her behavior is motherly, patting staff on the shoulder and calling them "ماما" (Mommy or dear). She is an energetic and dedicated leader whose personal circumstances and family situation allow her to dedicate much time to her work. However, she does face enormous challenges: the introduction of the new curriculum standards, parental dissatisfaction, and huge resistance to the reform from both the community and the media.
>
> Kawla is a relatively young leader in her late twenties who started her career as a PE teacher. Kawla focused more on organizational details, rules and regulations, whilst her assistant concentrated on people development and learning. Although Kawla wants to be involved in every aspect of her school, she is not around the school so often, instead spending most of her time in her office. Her main leadership challenges are fostering teamwork among her staff and coping with the pressure of being a cohort one school.
>
> Saeed is a very tall man in his late thirties, a soft-spoken and thoughtful leader who was eager to show me the best of his school. Many staff told me of the autonomy that Saeed's leadership permits. Saeed strives to create a school that increases the sense of community or family (a word he often uses) thereby dismantling the hierarchical arrangement of roles in the school. His school's main challenge is student behavior and "artificial workload".

Figure 6. The four main school leaders

Section 1: Leaders' perceptions of the reform and how those leaders are managing the implementation

The first and second research questions asked about school leaders' perceptions of the changes resulting from the *Education for a New Era* reform and their roles in managing the reform. In this section, I present leaders' perceptions and their roles in managing the change in order to address these two questions. The four main themes, as identified below, are illustrated with excerpts from the source data. They are presented in a descriptive manner to allow the leaders' voices to emerge.

Theme 1: Increasing responsibilities and workload

In this theme, I will present leaders' perceptions of workload, the reasons informing those perceptions, and their respective workload management strategies.

Leaders' perceptions of workload

The four leaders described their workload as especially 'heavy' at certain times, such as report writing or during assessment periods. At these times, their staff tended to become highly stressed, and the leaders believed that this had a negative effect upon staff performance. These negative perceptions appeared to be more prominent in the second school (Salwa's school), for three reasons. Firstly, this school's higher student number (relative to other schools) adds increased workload. Secondly, I observed one teacher sleeping on her desk and how teachers were actually running between meetings and classes. These observations illustrated the staff's experience of 'overload,' not only in a mental capacity, but also in a physical one. Thirdly, the staff had to work during their break times. At the end of the day they were acutely tired because they had not had a real break.

Workload did not only affect leaders' work inside the schools, but it impacted their personal lives too. All four leaders confirmed that they took work home to finish, and the main reasons for this were interruptions from teachers, the need to talk with colleagues, and having to attend unexpected meetings. However, sometimes the leaders managed to do a substantial amount of work at school with effective time management. Some adopted strategies such as staying later at school when it was quiet.

All female participants resented having to take work home, because it interfered with their home life. Salwa said, "My work does not finish at 2:00. I continue working at home. Although I have support at home, that school workload of course affects my responsibility as a mother." Kawla described the same lack of balance between work and life: "I stopped participating in social events because I have loads of stuff to finish." In the boys' school, Saeed explained, "Sometimes we have to come to school in the evening or finish some work during the weekend, but my situation is better than my wife's who is a teacher. Leaving the house in the evening for work is difficult." However, the situation in the boys' school seems to be less stressful than in the female-led school. Women are trying to manage both work and home responsibilities because of expectations that women should undertake all domestic responsibilities.

Reasons behind workload

In all the four schools, too much paperwork and data entry were the main contributors towards excessive workload. Leaders were burdened with increased levels of administrative tasks due to SEC demands for data. They found that they had been asked to submit extra reports, statistics, and paperwork, and remarked that their teachers needed to prepare files for each subject. Leaders reported perceptions of a lack of control over the nature and amount of their work, largely because they felt compelled to complete so much paperwork, which, in their view, did not benefit student learning.

Leaders found the extra paperwork frustrating. As Amna explained, "Every year we have new policies and decisions. They [i.e. the SEC] change the lesson plans, the books and the yearly plan." She said, "By 10:00 every morning my assistant has to send student and teacher absence records to the SEC." This task is time-consuming, and leaders viewed this daily reporting as pointless. Kawla said that there was no benefit to doing this task, and she believed that it simply increased workload. She stated: "What is the point of sending student numbers every single day? We can do it on a monthly basis and I'm not sure what the SEC is doing with all these forms." The constant changes in the reform policies and unnecessary paperwork caused extra workload. A study carried out by RAND to evaluate the progress of the reform on 16 schools over a period of two years from 2005 to 2007 found that school administrators reported that frequent policy changes had "fostered a sense of instability" (Constant et al., 2010, p. 459).

From the interviews, it seemed that paperwork in all the four schools was not a true measure of leaders' efforts. Saeed remarked: "Records are helpful, but sometimes it is not an accurate description of our actions. We can write something that we did not achieve or it could be the opposite: we could do something important without writing about it." Saeed gave a reason behind the demand for paperwork, saying: "The problem is that people who make decisions are far away from the reality, and are not fully aware of what is going on inside schools." One coordinator in Saeed's school added: "Most of our paperwork is for show only. So, when the SEC or the EI come they check our work. Some of this paperwork does not reflect our real work." The four leaders stated that the extra workload was caused by external requests from the SEC; however, internal factors inside schools also created more work. These factors will be explained in the following section.

Artificial workload

Timperley and Robinson (2000, p. 47) suggest, "Teachers not only suffer from workload problems but also create them." The findings from the present study support this statement. School leaders not only suffer from external workload pressures, but also create what Saeed describes as an "artificial workload":

> We have artificial loads. By this I mean that some leaders ask their team to do unnecessary tasks because they want to show who is boss. This adds a great burden to teachers. I am not saying we don't have a heavy workload, but coordinators can play a role in creating more and more work. (Saeed, personal communication, Janaury 9, 2012)

The role of department head is important, yet Saeed explained the role it can play in creating more work for others. This finding is similar to that of Timperley and Robinson (2000), who argue that "strong subject department identity" is likely to result in increased workload through fragmentation, duplication of effort, and the addition of new tasks to those already existing. In this study some heads of department requested unnecessary tasks, causing some evident staff tension.

Artificial workload occurs when leaders ask for unnecessary tasks to be performed, but it also occurs because these schools are obliged to participate in all the external programs and activities. Being a cohort one school affects leaders, since it adds pressure to participate in the SEC's and external organizations' activities. Salwa agreed, "we always have a heavy workload, because we aim for the best, and so we put pressure on our teachers!" Kawla also said:

> It is assumed that in cohort one, our students have already met specific standards. I feel we are bound to the institution we belong to, and we have been told that "Aljazeera" is always on top. We have met the standards, and we have to go even higher than that. The SEC asked all the schools from all the cohorts to participate in the science research program, so if you were in my position would you back out? (Kawla, personal communication, December 20, 2012)

Kawla felt that the school's reputation in the community required them to participate in all external activities. It was interesting to find out that being a cohort one school influenced the leaders' role. While the leaders frequently cited the importance of this designation, none of the teachers I spoke with made any mention of it. The schools have a strong commitment to external programs, and staff are required to participate in the provision of these activities. While leaders may support the school's vision on the involvement in extracurricular activities, for busy teachers the time required could affect their work inside the school.

The findings from this study show that the four principals believe the reform increases their workload. However, variations occur between the principals' perceptions of those reforms and those held by some of their followers. In each school, there were at least two subject coordinators who disagreed with the principals about workload. These coordinators felt a considerable degree of personal control over the amount of work, perceiving that their new role was achievable by effective organization of their new tasks. Also, having clearer instructions via the new policies helped them to accomplish their tasks on time. Finally, they believed that, by logical extension, the new reform would require them to participate in different activities and that, consequently, extra work was inevitable in the implementation of the change. Significantly, although all four principals agreed the workload was heavy, at least two staff members from each school disagreed with them. Participants were asked about which factors would make workload more manageable for themselves and for teachers. Their views will be presented in the next section.

Managing workload

The four school leaders were well aware of the extra work pressures existing for teachers. They sought to minimize these pressures but said that responding to the demands from the SEC was often difficult. For example, all the schools have to participate in extra-curricular activities and external programs. They also need to send daily documents to the SEC and must record their work in files.

The effective management of the teachers' workload was perceived by leaders as their primary responsibility. Leaders said they had taken steps to reduce their own workloads because of concerns about health effects or concerns about "work-life balance" (Marshall et al., 2012). Among these leaders is Amna, previously diagnosed with high blood pressure, who always attempted to finish all her work at school and not take it home. Another work-life balance strategy Amna mentioned was the importance of understanding the new policy. As she described, "We need clear policies and sometimes we receive these new changes in a critical time, I mean before assessment week or before school break." Salwa believed that prioritizing her tasks and managing her time were the best ways to manage the workload. She commented: "I understand that prioritizing tasks is helpful; I do the urgent task first, then the important ones and finally the things that can wait for a few days, but with constant changes and sudden meetings these seem impossible." Effective time management and organizational skills were the main strategies identified by participants as crucial to workload management. However, they also believe that clarifying instructions and some stability in policy decisions would contribute considerably to the same goal.

In sum, the four leaders believed that the reform increased their workload, both at school and outside. The ensuing amount of work was similar in both boys' and girls' schools, but the problems caused were worse in the latter because women also had additional responsibilities at home. Qatari society in the 21st century remains gendered. The society's gender-based norms are largely informed by traditional Islamic thought, as well as local custom, in which men and women fulfill distinct but complementary roles. Specifically, men are expected to financially support the household, while women carry out all of its day-to-day tasks. Under the present Amir,[1] His Highness Sheikh Hamad bin Khalifa Al Thani, many initiatives have encouraged Qatari women to take a more prominent role in public and professional life. Nevertheless, the expectations of Qatari society, as confirmed by my interviewees, demand that managing the private, domestic sphere remains the sole responsibility of Qatari women. Finally, leaders not only suffer from workload, but they also create it. Some leaders can manage to cope with their tasks, but others become more stressed by them. Clarity of instruction and stability in policies are two factors that can reduce the negative workload impact.

Theme 2: Collaboration

Collaboration is a key characteristic of school change and school success. Successful principals empower staff through collaboration. They encourage risk-taking and problem-solving (Davenport & Anderson, 2002). Leaders' perceptions of collabo-

---

(1) Present Amir of Qatar at the time of this study.

ration and their roles in fostering collaboration in their schools is addressed in this section, concluding with collaboration management strategies.

The meaning of a collaborative school

In order to present leaders' perceptions of collaboration, it is helpful to explain the meaning of a collaborative school first. Collaborative schools are places where the staff share their ideas, materials, problems and solutions in order to foster student learning by encouraging teamwork and collegiality (Peterson & Brietzke, 1994). The four schools in this study are organizations implementing a new reform and therefore need to work effectively together. In all four schools, the senior management appears to work well together and support each other. However, the problems occur specifically within each department. One or two departments from each school faced teamwork challenges. Sharing ideas and finding closer collaboration across departments was also weak. Teachers and the administration needed to work together to build a collaborative culture. Peterson and Deal (2002) called collaborative schools "positive schools" while labeling those which failed to collaborate as "toxic schools." Table 3 shows the features of both schools.

However, this contrast between the positive and the toxic is somewhat uncommon, and perhaps, in an educational context, an inappropriate association. Toxicity commonly denotes lethal contamination. Certainly, in the case of my own research, while each of the four schools observed does undoubtedly display certain negative features, none of them is so irredeemably flawed as to merit the label 'toxic'. A redefinition of terms may be required, in which the counterpart to "positive schools" may, for instance, be conceptualized as "less collaborative schools". I am here drawing inspiration from the response of one participant, Omar, the assistant to Saeed who leads the boys' school. Omar chooses to reframe change 'resisters' as 'less motivated staff'.

Positive schools	Toxic schools
1. Teachers regularly engage in professional dialogue with colleagues; share ideas, knowledge, and techniques; and participate in collaborative problem-solving around classroom issues.	1. Teachers work largely alone in their rooms, interacting little with their colleagues and keeping problems of practice to themselves.
2. Teachers work together to develop shared technical knowledge and discover common solutions to challenging problems.	2. Teachers feel separated from one another, seldom engaging their peers in conversation, professional sharing, or problem-solving.

Table 3. Positive and toxic schools, adapted from Peterson and Deal (2002)

The findings from this study will be discussed based on these two definitions from Peterson and Deal (2002). Also, it is important to note here that the data presented includes that gained both from the four main principals and from their respective team members.

Positive examples

Undoubtedly, each of the themes considered by the present research interacts with the others. For example, collaboration, when not managed effectively, can certainly lead to increased workload as an unforeseen (and, arguably, highly detrimental) by-product. Some leaders and teachers viewed themselves as learners. They saw teacher training as providing opportunities for professional growth. Some new teachers did not have problems attending training workshops inside and outside the school. They consider these opportunities to learn from each other. As one teacher said, "I'm learning a lot from the more experienced teachers, because I'm a new teacher."

Schlectly (2002) argues that teachers working together on teaching tasks are likely to learn together to improve the quality of their work, which leads to higher student engagement. Little (2003) also states that when teachers "collectively question ineffective teaching routines, examine new conceptions of teaching and learning, find generative ways to acknowledge and respond to conflict, and engage in actively supporting one another's professional growth," this process strengthens teaching and learning (p. 923). In my study, teachers also reported that sharing experiences was helpful for their professional learning. I observed that teachers sometimes discussed new ideas and shared experiences within the same department. In Amna's school, there was evidence of teachers in the same department working collaboratively as a team. Heads of department held discussions with their teachers, sharing "best practices." Teachers confirmed that sharing best practices with other teachers and their coordinators helped to improve the quality of their work.

Team collaboration was also evident in the second school (Salwa's school) in certain departments. This occurred, for example, in the English department. An experienced English teacher attended the staff meeting during the absence of her coordinator, and she communicated the management's instructions to the English department team. It was a good example of the English coordinator's efforts to build her team's capacities: she had a good relationship with her team and she was trying to build their professional skills. The staff discussed and scheduled regular weekly meetings and lesson plan meetings. They shared ideas and stories about student accomplishment or teaching methods. Collegial relationships were observed through staff humor and jokes.

Teachers also identified observation of other teachers' classroom practice as a helpful factor in their professional learning. They valued the opportunity to observe other teachers in their same area or subject. All the four principals encouraged their departments to exchange visits and learn from each other. They all believed that through collaboration between departments and sharing ideas, teachers would improve their teaching skills. Saeed said, "I always encourage visits between teachers. In these visits, teachers learn and share their teaching practices."

Another kind of collaboration was teachers' discussions in the hallways between lessons. For example, science teachers would converse with other science teachers in this way. Most of them would talk quickly during the five minutes between classes and break time. Teachers talked together periodically to coordinate how they were covering a specific teaching unit and to share successful teaching strategies. Learning from the practices of others was valued as important. However, equally important is the reflection, discussion and internalization of these practices. When I talked to some teachers about sharing ideas, none reported how their lessons would be improved because of this collaboration. Instead, what they reported to me was a more general appreciation of this sharing. Schools need to create a culture such that teachers can reflect on these professional development (PD) sessions and their impacts on students.

In the boys' school led by Saeed, the participants considered the professional development program to be a support, and the school seemed flexible about hours spent on it. In the girls' schools, however, the participants were anxious about PD and considered it negatively because it affected their evaluation. The development program required them to attend for a specific number of hours and stay back after school ended. Thus, schools and leaders played an important role in implementing policies handed down by the SEC. There is a difference between centralized SEC requirements and the requirements imposed by each school on its teachers and students. Each school's interpretation of the requirements increasing the "artificial workload" is mentioned in Theme 1.

Negative examples

The four principals were aware that staff collaboration within some departments was a problem. Amna said: "I am aware that some departments in my school don't work well together. The reform required them to work as a team; this is a new concept, but with time, this will be improved." Salwa understood that working as a team was vital to bring about a more successful implementation of the reform. In her school, the new math department coordinator was experiencing teamwork problems. Salwa believed that she herself as a principal needed to work to solve that problem.

Suffian, the science coordinator in Saeed's school, and Raesa, the Arabic coordinator in Kawla's school, appeared to be the coordinators under the most stress, due to lack of teacher collaboration and, in Raesa's case, lack of experience in team leadership. She said, "My team doesn't listen to me, so I go to Miss Lwloa (the vice-principal) and she sends an official request to them. This is the only way that they can respond to me." She received support from her senior team, but the support seemed more emotional than strategic. Long-term confidence building to deal with conflict would appear more prudent than her current temporary solutions.

Sometimes, a team works well, but the problem is their relationship with their coordinator. The English department in the first school, led by Amna, had this problem. Nadia, the English coordinator, has teaching and leadership experience, but her staff complained about her leadership style. I met the English teachers in their meeting room. I had just introduced myself, and immediately I was struck by their openness. They reported mistreatment and criticism they received from their head. Maha said, "We don't feel supported and appreciated like teachers in other departments." Nevertheless, their coordinator, Nadia, reported a good relationship with her team. In some cases, such as this one, there appears to be a contrast between what the heads of department believed, and how teachers actually felt. Leaders play an important role in creating a positive or toxic culture in schools, as will be discussed in detail in the next section.

Leaders' roles in fostering collaboration

Successful principals "build collaboration internally and build strong relationships outside the school community" (Day et al.,

2010, p. 4). The participants in this study acknowledged the need to build relationships with their staff inside the school, and with the SEC, parents, and the wider community outside the school. Salwa said, "I have a good relationship with my team; they are like a family to me." This observation was clear when I observed how she dealt and communicated with her team. She stated, "We all have workload problems and I am trying to support my staff." When I asked her about how she built her team, she said, "It is my responsibility to show my team, especially those who previously worked in the MoE, the benefits of the new system and support them." Salwa added that it was important to build good relationships, saying, "We all work here together as a team. We respect each other and I don't like giving orders; I always discuss things with my teachers." The four leaders believed that collaboration is important; however, they faced problems between members that could cause difficulties. This is a situation identified by Fullan (2002) as one of the most difficult skills for educational leaders.

A leader's role in team building is critical. McLaughlin and Talbert (2001) agree on the importance of the department heads' role in building professional community among teachers, who can be involved in activities such as sharing ideas, developing assignments and programs of work, and discussing teaching strategies. These activities contribute powerfully to professional learning. Anwar, the math coordinator in Saeed's school, had been teaching for over 20 years, and he had influenced the culture of the math department. He set an example of collaborative working relationships, encouraged working in teams, and created an environment of collective openness to new ideas.

Teachers also have a role in developing collaborative culture. As Johnson (1990) notes:

> Teachers themselves must ultimately take responsibility for collaboration. Teachers both constitute and create the context for collegiality. Removing the structural barriers to exchange will not alone ensure that teachers eagerly and confidently cooperate and critique each other's practice. Strong norms

of autonomy and privacy prevail among teachers. Creeping fears of competition, exposure to shortcomings, and discomfiting criticism often discourage open exchange, cooperation, and growth. Until teachers overcome such fears and actively take charge of their own professional relations, teaching will likely remain isolating work. (1990, pp. 178–179)

The fears described by Johnson (1990) may be present in teachers such as Fadia, a math teacher in Salwa's school, who constructed a barrier to collaboration with new coordinator Samia. These fears may also be present in Raesa's team (in Kawla's school) and Suffian (in Saeed's school), where teachers appeared resistant to instructions as well as to efforts towards open and constructive communication.

I observed a substantial amount of non-collaborative work in the science department in Saeed's school; Suffian suffered from a lack of team collaboration and was not comfortable working with his team. He seemed very stressed, highly anxious, and prone to being short-tempered. Lack of a supportive team prevented him from effectively coping with the change. His teachers reacted negatively to some orders or requests, and this affected their working relationships. Suffian said: "I am aware that my team do[es]n't work well together. I always encourage them to share and to learn from each other. But still I have difficulties with some teachers." Suffian's team members were less motivated and less committed to working together.

The findings from this study also showed examples of positive collaboration. Basma, the Early Years coordinator in Salwa's school, had a strong team. She confirmed collaboration as a requirement for a successful department, stating: "I have 10 teachers. At the beginning I was worried about how to work with them, but they work as a team, and for me as a leader this makes many things easier. Sometimes they have issues but we're able to solve them internally." Similarly, in Saeed's school, Ahmed was proud of his team, saying: "I have been working with my team for more than six years. We are friends more than colleagues;

we support each other. And honestly we are cooperative. I have a very good team. Sometimes we disagree but we work well together." Clearly, team building is a shared undertaking, coming from both leaders and their team. A good relationship between the team members can help in facilitating the leaders' role in managing change.

Collaboration management

It is well acknowledged in business management that attitudes are contagious. Likewise, a school leader promoting the change at school has to 'sell' it to staff so that they 'buy into' the change. This process involves emotional affiliation. Humans are adept at detecting commitment and sincerity, or, on the other hand, fakery and opportunism. A critical component of 'walking the talk' (i.e. putting into practice professional management discourse) is a leader's sincere demonstration of his or her loyalty and commitment to the change concept. When such loyalty is perceived clearly by the staff, the likely outcome (at least according to my own observation and professional practice) is greater staff motivation to implement such changes. In this sense, while many aspects of change are multidirectional processes, the top-down (leader to staff) direction of motivation remains crucial to the change's successful implementation.

Since change involves learning to adopt new attitudes and beliefs, it is necessarily a slow process (Fullan, 1999). Moreover, change requires a leader who is able to build a team. Team members are also required to support each other in dealing with the change. All the four leaders agreed on the importance of leaders' skills in team relationship building. Amna commented: "Change takes time and in order to help others with the change, we have to choose the right leader to lead the team, so that they can help to transfer positive attitudes to the rest of the team." Belief in change and a positive approach to the reform also contribute to leaders' successful change implementation. One coordinator said: "I have to believe in the worth of the change. I have to convince the others that it is important and I have to explain it and show them the advantages of doing it. This is the way we work as a team." Another explained, "When I believe in the change then I have the ability to convince my team to implement the new policy." It was interesting to observe that most of the senior managers had been working together for six to ten years, which seems to reflect their personal and professional commitment as strongly linked to longevity and affective social ties. Vital in this long-term team building and staff retention is the role of the leader; without a supportive and effective leader, teachers would likely migrate to employment with other schools.

Leaders play an important role in solving problems and explaining new policies to assist the team's understanding of what they need to implement. The English coordinator in Salwa's school, Maryam, described her experience in this way: "It took me time to build my team, and sometimes I have to contact them outside school hours. At the beginning it was hard for all of us but now we understand each other. I have to simplify things for them in order to help them understand the new policy and convince them to implement it more successfully. Of course, it's hard to change things that we are used to doing, but showing them how this can be beneficial for the students can help to convince them." Similarly, Randa in Amna's school said, "Once I understood what I was supposed to do, it made things easier for me. Also, as a leader I have to simplify things for my teachers. If I only give orders, they won't do what they're supposed to do. And that's the reason why some departments are not working well. I have to convince them of the benefits of the change by building good relationships, and that makes things work as a team." Change requires efforts from both groups and individuals to work well together.

Building a team requires a good leader and team members who support collaborative work. Saeed said, "I don't like individual decision-making; I prefer to talk with my team. We discuss matters together and come up with one conclusion: this makes implementation much easier." Another coordinator proudly stated: "I have to understand my team, and consider their personal problems. I have to encourage them and support them. We have been working together for a long time, which has helped me to understand each one. My team doesn't follow my orders because I am their coordinator, but because we have a good working relationship." This approach was clear when I observed how the coordinator dealt with and talked with his team in their weekly meetings. He asked for their advice and consulted them.

Hence, research into school culture, change, and improvement finds that success is more likely when teachers are collegial and work collaboratively on improvement activities (Levine & Lezotte, 1990; Fullan & Hargreaves, 1991). Collegial relationships among and between staff are an important feature of those collaborative schools more successful in implementing the reform. When teachers and administrators work together, the level of commitment, energy, and motivation is likely to be higher and the reforms thus more easily implemented. In the all the four schools, the senior management are working well as a unit; however, each school is struggling with collaboration in one or two departments.

Theme 3: The emotional responses to change

Change occurs in management for various reasons. The catalysts could be positive events or negative ones, such as when people anticipate or experience emotional gains and losses (Huy, 2002), when there is uncertainty (French, 2001), or when processes are perceived as too quick, too slow, or too frequent (Smollan, Sayers & Matheny, 2010). Duignan (2006) identifies the key challenges for educational leaders to be ones involving complex and often conflicting human relationships. He calls them "the ones that keep educational leaders awake at night" (2006, p. 42). The strategies used by the leaders in this study are similar and reflect emotional resilience skills identified in the literature. This section outlines leaders' emotional responses to change and the strategies I used to collect the data. Finally, I present how the leaders managed their emotions.

Identifying the emotional responses to change

Crawford (2007, p. 89) states that "research in emotions is difficult, both in access to people and their memory of events." Research in emotions is problematic for several reasons. Firstly, people may not wish to reveal their true feelings. Secondly, they may not have the vocabulary or terminology to adequately express their feelings. Finally, people isolate their difficult feelings and project them elsewhere as a social defence. Yet this sort of research is important in the present context to understand the link between introducing new reform changes and how this impacts emotions. In general, emotional responses were clearer in the observations than in the interviews.

In this study, identifying emotional responses proved challenging and thus necessitated a systematic method encompassing semantic and non-verbal communication. Firstly, I took detailed notes about participants' descriptions of incidents they had experienced. For example, Kawla was angry when she talked about her difficulties with parents at the beginning of the reform. Saeed plainly expressed anger and disappointment when he talked about solving student behavior problems at the police station. Secondly, the leaders' body language and gestures gave an indication of their feelings. For example, the interview with Amna ended in tears and was a very distressing interview, her reaction to which reflected her emotions. Finally, their emotions were visible from their direct reactions or responses to events or conversations. I observed that Salwa was experiencing a sense of "loss of control" when she was interrupted by her staff.

Crawford (2009, p. 8) differentiates between three types of behavior arising from emotions: feelings (what we experience internally), emotions (feelings that we show), and moods (feelings that persist over time). Most of my analysis is on emotion, although feelings and mood also play a part in the discussion. For example, Amna showed her emotion when expressing anger and disappointment talking about her working relationship with the SEC. However, in the case of Salwa's loss of emotional control, her mood and response were related to her underlying approach to work and her response to the change over time.

Types of emotions

Positive emotions about the reform

Throughout the schools' portraits, it is apparent that leaders responded to change differently. Some leaders described their experience of change positively: Amna, for example, professed to "enjoy the idea of the reform," while Salwa said, "I feel satisfied to see my team are managing their problems." These responses demonstrated a positive feeling of pride and a sense of accomplishment with reform. One coordinator said, "Students now use more problem-solving skills than in the previous system and this is a good thing." Positive emotions were conveyed in their expressions and speech about the reform.

Salwa felt positive about the change, and this in turn had a positive impact on her work. Despite working in a stressful environment, as a leader she was trying to provide support for her team and to reduce stress. When the school lacked a PE teacher, Salwa undertook these duties; similarly, when a librarian was required, she carried out the role. She positively promoted the reform, on its arrival, among her staff, reminding herself and others: "We joined these schools ourselves—we chose the hard work."

Another example of a positive emotional response was when teachers felt trusted by their leaders. It seems reasonable that for leaders successfully to implement the reform, trust is a prerequisite. I observed that in the first and last hours of each school day, some teachers in Saeed's school appeared relaxed and free from anxiety. This mood was in sharp contrast with the girls' schools, where staff became stressed about being in the school at 7:00 a.m. sharp. In the girls' school they used an electronic finger signature to 'clock in,' whereas the boys' school used handwritten signatures. Saeed's teachers expressed their appreciation of their principal's trust.

The thumbprint registration technique for staff is a recent trend in Qatari schools. Although not mandatory, it has gained some popularity, perhaps one of the strongest indicators of individual school leadership style and organizational trust in this study. Bottery (2004) suggests three principal foundations for trust: first, an agreement on values and value priorities; second, people doing what they say they are going to do; and third, perceptions of employee competence. Meanwhile, Hoy and Tschannen-Moran (1999) study the impact of trust on school organizations and student achievement, describing trust as "an individual's or group's willingness to be vulnerable to another party based on the confidence that the latter party is benevolent, reliable, competent, honest, and open" (1999, p. 186). Their definition identifies five characteristics of people or groups who are trusted: benevolence, reliability, competency, honesty, and openness. Saeed believed that his staff were overburdened, so he acted with benevolence towards them and always tried to consider their well-being. He could rely on them to be on time and do their work. He said: "Staff members are burdened enough. I trust them, and I assume that they will come and leave on time. Some teachers leave early, but this is often because they do not have a last lesson in the timetable."

Negative emotions due to reform

Crawford (2009) indicates a leadership paradox inherent in a school's professional demands: complex emotions are invoked through leadership activity, and yet leaders are expected not to display these. Some leaders in this study showed negative emotions to include tears and frustration in dealing with challenges—yet their role requires them to appear calm. Participants use words like 'frustrated,' 'angry,' and 'upset' to describe their feelings during difficult situations. Two leader interviews ended with the participants in tears. The first such interview took place with Amna, the principal, who did not feel appreciated by the SEC for all her efforts when faced with the requirements of the reform. She reported feeling "frustration when being controlled by the

SEC," and she suffered due to lack of autonomy. Meanwhile, the Arabic coordinator, Aisha, was exhausted and overwhelmed by her workload and her responsibilities as a mother. Lawrence-Lightfoot (1983) argues that empathy is key to good data collection because there is "the need to experience and reflect upon one's feelings in order to successfully identify with another's perspective" (1983, p. 370). My role in this study as an outsider, together with my own previous experience of being head of department while a mother, assisted my understanding of these female leaders' feelings in dealing with change in the work environment, particularly when combined with all the duties and demands of motherhood.

Stress as a negative emotion was mentioned earlier in workload and collaboration themes. In this study, individual stress was mainly brought on by heavy workload and a lack of collaboration from other team members. Kyriacou (2001) defines stress in an instructional context as "the experience by a teacher of unpleasant, negative emotions, such as anger, anxiety, tension, frustration or depression, resulting from some aspect of their work as a teacher" (2001, p. 28). Some heads of department expressed their negative emotions about being responsible for an uncollaborative team: this was a situation experienced by Suffian, the science coordinator in the boys' school, who appeared very stressed and highly anxious. Travers and Cooper (1996) suggest sources of teacher stress: time pressure and workload, coping with change, dealing with colleagues, and poor working conditions. Heads of department could also cause negative feelings. In Amna's school, the relationship between the head of English and her teachers caused anger and hurt feelings, with the English teachers showing anger and frustration from lack of leader support. Fullan (2002) agrees that bad relationships and spread of negative emotions are both obstacles to developing an effective school. Unsatisfactory leader–team relationships were responsible for creating an emotionally unpleasant situation.

Negative emotions affect teachers' sense of well-being. Some teachers expressed their concern at the constant requests from inside and outside the school. One female teacher described her state of constant stress due to repeated requests from the school management and the SEC. With four children at home, she struggled to balance her professional and parenting roles, explaining: "I've become too nervous and stressed because I don't like to talk with people outside the school. I was also losing hair because of the stress. I have become isolated and I need time to be alone and to rest." Juggling in this manner can take a toll on teachers' well-being and their performance as teachers due to lack of work-life balance. Three teachers in Kawla's school complained of being tired and stressed, even experiencing health problems caused by stress. Work-life balance has been explored in different contexts, including higher education (Marshall et al., 2012), the medical field (Keeton, Fenner, Johnson, & Hayward, 2007) and the construction industry (Watts, 2009). In an effort to attain a better work-life balance, some leaders (discussed in the workload theme) worked to manage their time and prioritize responsibilities. However, some leaders struggled to have a balance while juggling multiple roles. Leadership strategies for managing emotions will be discussed in the next section.

Managing emotions

When the leaders were asked about mechanisms they used to manage stress and frustration, they did not specify emotional intelligence or resilience but instead mentioned skills related to emotional resilience. Emotional resilience is described as "the capacity to withstand and renew oneself in the light of life stressors, thrive and make meaning from the challenge" (Flin, 1996, p. 8). The data provides clear evidence of the link between the coping mechanisms described by participants and their emotional control. Observations showed some subject coordinators were available when needed by their teachers, such as before mothers' meetings and assessment week, which made them feel better. Ultimately, these connections and team work contribute to a better teaching and learning atmosphere.

Some coordinators demonstrated the importance of emotional control through remaining calm under pressure. Some felt that their emotional resilience had developed through dealing with challenging situations. The findings illustrate the correlation between the leaders' emotional resilience and their ability to cope with the change. Randa, for example, was smiling and calm, and her personality was reflected in the way she led her team. Although she experienced departmental challenges, mainly due to regular teacher turnover, she explained her coping mechanisms as follows: "Sometimes I have teachers without teaching experience and I have to support them, step by step, then everything will go well." Randa's emotional resilience and her ability to stay focused were invaluable in helping her to cope.

Emotional resilience was a topic that emerged centrally in many interviews. Reham, the English coordinator in Kawla's school, and Anwar, the math coordinator in the boys' school, both described the need to demonstrate positive and confident role-modeling in dealing with difficulties. Both were calm leaders, and their emotional responses were reflected in their team management style. In dealing with teachers resistant to change, their strategies featured ways to sidestep staff anger and frustration, a practice consistent with Beatty's (2002) observation that emotional resilience can develop and sustain relationships especially with teachers who resist change.

What is not explored in this study is why some leaders are able to manage and deal with implementation problems while others faced with the same challenges are unable to cope. The leaders in this study all deal with their own challenges and some demonstrate the ability to manage complex situations. What is also unclear from the research is whether or not emotional intelligence can be learned. Groves, McEnrue and Shen (2008) called for leaders to be trained in emotional intelligence. The need for leadership development that supports the emotional dimension of leadership cannot be overestimated and has implications for experienced and inexperienced leaders alike.

Finally, emotions can be positive or negative and those of leaders play an important role in change management. Their teachers already have a compelling reason to make that change a success; however, they are fighting a constant battle because of the varying ways in which they struggle with its implementation, due to lack of clarity in regard to appropriate methods. This affects other areas of their professional and personal lives, resulting in increased stress, diminished focus, and an ensuing lack of value ascribed by teachers to the requested change. Leaders have solutions in place to deal with change initiated by their own schools; however, the change that comes from the SEC has not been clarified in terms of processes and procedures. These factors, therefore, make everyone's job harder and their acceptance of change incredibly difficult.

Theme 4: Conditions for change

This section outlines the various conditions needed by leaders and their teams to implement the reform. In it, I discuss constant change as a factor that hinders leaders' roles and their ability to effectively facilitate the implementation of change. Finally, I discuss the varying roles of leaders within both the facilitation and the implementation of change.

Leaders' perceptions of conditions for change

The four leaders agreed upon the importance of providing positive conditions to enable their teachers to work more successfully. Some leaders reduced the teaching load, and provided teaching resources, space for teachers and information when needed. Implementing change takes time. As Ely (1999) puts it: "The implementers must have time to learn, adapt, integrate, and reflect on what they are doing. The innovation needs time for the implementers to understand the innovation and develop the abilities to adapt it" (1999, p. 4). Most of the leaders featured in this study also tried to provide encouragement and time for teachers to finish their work.

The study's findings on conditions for change will follow the structure of Ely's conditions, keeping in mind the implementation phase of the reform. Ely (1990) refers to "conditions of change" as the environmental factors affecting the implementation of the change process. Ely's model proposes several conditions, such as sufficient knowledge and skills, availability of resources, participation, commitment, and leadership, that can help change agents to cope with the change process more successfully. Ely's conditions for change are explained below:

Sufficient knowledge and skills

In order to make the implementation successful, "the people who will ultimately implement any innovation must possess sufficient knowledge and skills to do the job" (Ely, 1999, p. 4). Without enough training of implementers in the effective use of new tools or techniques, the processes of innovation will soon wither, and may peter out altogether. The school leaders I observed demonstrated provision of sufficient professional development inside the school and training at the SEC. Salwa stated, "I always encourage internal and external visits between teachers so they can learn from each other." Similarly, Kawla noted: "We have training for both new teachers and the more experienced staff. Also, we have training for the management staff. Most of this training is provided by the SEC and by other external companies." Although schools provide training for staff, some teachers found it a challenge rather than a support. In the girls' schools, the participants were anxious about the PD program's effect on their evaluation. The development program required them to attend for a specific number of hours and stay back after school time. In the boys' schools, however, PD was viewed by the staff as being supportive, and the school seemed flexible about the hours spent on it. Saeed, the principal of the boys' school, stated that the quality of training was more important than the number of hours spent attending professional development that was often not beneficial for the staff. He said:

> I am against any training that adds to teacher workloads. If the teacher has training every week, how can he use what he has learned in his lessons? Focus should be on the quality of the PD [and] not the quantity. In some schools they compete about how many hours teachers spent on the training. (Saeed, personal communication, January 9, 2012)

These findings correspond with those of other studies including that of Zellman et al. (2009, p. 50) on the implementation of the reform in Qatari schools, which found that school teachers reported feeling "overwhelmed and burned out" by the number of required training hours. Additionally, a study carried out by Nasser and Romanowski (2011), which considered the impact of professional training on teachers in Qatari schools, found that one-third of the 49 teachers answering their survey felt the PD plan to be useful (2011, p. 162). However, the majority surveyed expressed disappointment and frustration with the content and organization of PD activities offered by their schools. Workshops were described as "haphazard, and did not build on a framework of activities that improved teaching," or lacking "logical flow or continuity" (2011, p. 162). Many teachers believed "the PD was run using a top-down approach in which teachers were generally coerced into school PD" (2011, p. 166) and had been "forced to conform to a set of expectations alien to their own needs" (2011, p. 165). To conclude, although training and professional development are important, they can occaasionally create extra work as expressed by teachers and leaders in this study.

Availability of resources

An innovation without appropriate resources to support its implementation, such as budget, tools, and materials, will not be successful. In my observations, the teachers in all four schools were satisfied with the resources available to them. Each classroom had an overhead projector and television and video equipment. Teachers had open access to stationery and most other teaching requirements. Computers were available in classrooms and in dedicated computer rooms. One teacher stated, "We have all the resources we need. If we need something for specific lessons, we request it through our coordinator. We have enough room; it's good because I can put my own things out." Teachers also had desks in a shared staffroom. However, the staffroom in the second school was crowded. The student numbers had increased, so the school converted the language lab into a staffroom. The increase in classroom size is quite a challenge for the school, increasing teachers' workloads per class and affecting teaching strategies and classroom management. That said, the coordinators were well satisfied with the levels of support available to them from their senior managers. They had access to the school secretarial staff and photocopying, but they said that more support in the form of typing and data entry was needed. Kawla commented: "I meet with the coordinators and always ask for their suggestions. If it's the case that we lack resources, I try to provide them myself or try to borrow them from other schools." In the boys' school, Saeed said, "We have a good budget to provide resources for our teachers." Girls' school leader Amna remembered the past: "Compared with the MoE system, we have enough resources for the library and science lessons." Resources are thus perceived across all four schools to have a central role in delivering innovation in the form of reform implementation.

It emerged that staff required encouragement in the performance or use of innovation in order to effectively implement or promote it. Saeed and Salwa were observed to focus on rewards for their staff. Recall what Saeed noted in his interview: "From what I am telling you, you might be thinking that we do this for show, but I know our staff want to stay here because we always appreciate their efforts." Salwa, too, confirmed her school's provision of rewards and incentives for teachers who had "gone the extra mile," especially those participating in extracurricular activities.

Participation

Participants should be encouraged to become involved in decision-making. In my study all stakeholders from staff to teachers to parents to students and leaders are participants in the reform. With opportunities to communicate their ideas and opinions, participants can have a sense of ownership of innovation (Ely, 1999). Teamwork is more likely to be effective when those responsible for implementation are included in a shared decision-making process (Scribner, Sawyer, Watson & Myers, 2007). Decision-making is essential to build a collaborative team, and yet involving the staff in decision-making was observed to be a problem in all the four schools.

Typically, in the Qatari context, decision-making is a top-down process rather than a collaborative one. In this study, reform-related decisions are made firstly by the SEC, and then at an individual school level by the school principal. This process is consistent with the general pattern of decision-making behavior in Qatar, where employees' suggestions and ideas are not solicited by the highest status holder.

While the ENE reform aims, among other requirements, to include school leaders in decision-making, in practice, such behavioral change is not rapid among leaders. Nevertheless, the Qatari school leaders observed tried to involve their team in any way that they could in the policy implementation process. Saeed agreed with the importance of involving his team in decision-making, stating: "I like to involve my teachers and to talk with them. I prefer this because it will convince them. And they can implement new decisions easier this way." Amna equally strived to involve her senior managers and teachers as much as possible in the decision-making process. Her assistant reported, "It is important to involve teachers in decision-making because it helps them to have ownership of the change." However, the final decision is always with the school principal. One of her staff commented: "We give our opinions, but in the end it is their decision." From my observations in the two weekly meetings between the principal and the other leaders, the leaders always looked to the principal for the final word. This process may give an appearance of staff participation in decisions, although the staff themselves may disagree with this assumption.

Leaders need to actively involve the team in decision-making. In order to realize successful change, those on the receiving end must be consulted in order to promote ownership of, and loyalty to, the cause (Paton & McCalman, 2008). Kawla added, "I tried to involve my staff in decision-making, but most of the time decisions were imposed by the SEC and I myself don't have any authority to be involved." Raesa, a coordinator in Kawla's school, said, "My role is like being a messenger. I inform my teachers about the management's decisions. I receive decisions from the management, and then I meet with my teachers to tell them about the decisions." Here, their role is implementation only.

Teachers and heads of department need to see the value of their undertakings because it affects their response to new policies. Teachers in this study follow orders and they have no option but to do as they are told. In order to sustain these changes, teachers need to be involved in decision-making and must see the benefit of implementing the new reform. One of leaders' many significances is as change agents; when leaders view themselves as agents of reform, they need to be aware of the improvements needed to make their leadership more effective (Fullan, 2006). Leaders in this study viewed themselves as implementers only, and some teachers did not have a sense of themselves as part of a larger reform or think about their role's contribution to "the big picture." Fullan (2006) emphasizes leaders' efforts to generate "organizational learning" in order to achieve sustainability: they aim "to generate more and more leaders who could think and act with the bigger picture in mind thereby changing the context within which people work in order to go beyond individual and team learning to organizational learning and system change" (2006, p. 121).

Commitment

Since implementation takes effort and time, implementers need to make a commitment. There must be "firm and visible evidence that there is endorsement and continuing support for implementation" (Ely, 1999, p. 5). All the leaders were committed to the change; however, their commitment was not shared by some members of their team. Leaders as implementers also need conditions to help make the reform successful, including a committed team and collaboration between staff. However, in some situations, leaders themselves need support in order to support their team. As Kawla commented: "I understand that my staff need support, but at the same I need their help too." Salwa additionally stressed the importance of her leadership role as a link between teachers and heads of department, in order to understand their needs and provide support. Saeed also added that encouraging his team and rewarding them is crucial to maintaining a committed staff. Leaders provide conditions to facilitate change, but as implementers they also need conditions.

Leadership

Leader commitment greatly influences the process of implementation. Leadership also includes the availability of effective support throughout the process. Saeed clearly had strong support from his staff. Their statements demonstrate this support: "The principal is absolutely wonderful, he's very supportive and the staff knows it; [the principal] has high standards but he doesn't push people. He has an open-door policy that is genuine. You can just walk in [to his office] at any time." Further, "he is very supportive and easy to communicate with." The teachers interviewed commented that the middle managers provided strong support, particularly with the curriculum standards, and believed that the subject coordinators work extremely hard to provide resource materials and curriculum assistance. One teacher confirms: "I know that I can go to my coordinator at any time for help. He's well organized and provides lots of resources."

Leaders also support their teams with both work-related problems and emotional support on issues in their personal lives. Reham said:

> I always show my team that I'm available for them when they need me. This gives the teachers confidence in coping

with all these changes. I also provide support for them, especially when we have to implement a new policy. I try to reduce other tasks. And the most important point is to consider their other personal issues or problems. (Reham, personal communication, December 19, 2011)

Further, leaders play an important role in facilitating change, as Sarah stated:

It's my personality; I can convince my team by showing them the positive side of any change. Sometimes they are annoyed and overloaded, so I can change my plan of action. But when we have a deadline it's difficult, because nothing is in my hands. What is in my hands is the way I put it to them. I know and I am confident that my teachers will give me the work and submit it on time. (Sarah, personal communication, December 25, 2011)

However, contradictions emerged between interview data and my observations. Leaders provided sufficient resources and time to implement new policies, while senior management had a good relationship with the heads of department. In the first school, the teachers, when describing their working environments in general said that they felt respected and valued. Blase and Blase (2002) found that mistreatment of teachers by principals had significant effects and classroom consequences. As a researcher, I decided to try to obtain more information on this sensitive issue, using as much tact and diplomacy as possible. I asked the Head of English very carefully about her support for her team. Although her response showed her confidence that she was providing sufficient support for them, her teachers' interviews previously obtained contradicted this view. They felt frustrated and lacking in support.

The importance of Ely's conditions may not be consistent over time, depending on individual and organizational stages of change implementation. Adopter perception can be influenced by their stages of concern (Hall & Hord, 1987) and experience and knowledge (Dooley, 1999; Ravitz, 1999; Sherry, Billig,

Stavalin, and Gibson, 2000). The study's four main leaders have been implementing the reform for more than eight years, while their perceptions of the importance of their conditions vary with the stages of implementation. For example, leadership and commitment are described as being more important than resources at the later stages of implementation.

In addition to Ely's model overlapping with this study, Bolman and Deal (2003) describe leadership under four frames of leadership styles that enhance our understanding of leadership. They developed these frames to show the way leaders think and act in response to everyday issues:

- The human resource frame focuses attention on human needs.
- The structural frame focuses on organizational goals and efficiency.
- The political frame emphasizes competition for scarce resources.
- The symbolic frame focuses on imagery, symbols and culture (Bolman & Deal, 2003).

Effective leaders and organizations rely on multiple frames and perspectives; there is always more than one way to respond to any organizational problem or dilemma (Bolman & Deal, 1991). Another researcher whose work provides valuable insights is Kotter, who has studied successful and unsuccessful change in organizations around the world. In his book *The Heart of Change* (2002), he argues that many change initiatives fail when change agents focus on reasons and structure and neglect human, political and symbolic elements (Bolman & Deal, 2003). In the present study, leaders use human and structural frames only, and they are observed trying to be responsive to teacher needs and goals to gain their commitment and loyalty. Effective human resource leaders listen well and communicate personal warmth and openness, and these qualities were evident when the four principals worked with their teams. However, staff should be empowered more through participation. As structural leaders, these professionals focus on tasks, facts and logic, but not on personality or emotions. It would seem useful and necessary to encourage and train school leaders to use not only the human resource and the structural frames but also to use the political and the symbolic frames. Leaders in the four schools work under the supervision of the SEC, a centralized institution, so it is difficult for them to exercise the networking, coalition building, and compromise negotiations, lacking the necessary bases of power required for the political framework (Bolman & Deal, 1991). Moreover, in a centralized education system, the principals cannot exercise the visionary leadership characteristic of the symbolic frame.

As explained in the above section, leaders are trying in various ways to provide adequate conditions for their followers to implement the reform. However, some factors could hinder successful implementation. These could be internal obstacles such as resistance to change that will be discussed under Theme 5 (Overall perceptions of challenges). External factors, such as constantly changing school policies, may also play a role, and it is these factors which are discussed in the next section.

Constant change: a significant obstacle to change implementation

Although leaders try to provide conditions to help teachers to work effectively, constant change in school policies sometimes affects their working status negatively. Leaders are working in a school context that is, by its nature, dynamic, complex and unpredictable. All four schools face constant change in the SEC policies and leaders experience this as confusing. Some teachers worry about whether they are giving their best to their students. Salwa differentiated between two types of change, identifying some as helpful and contributing to improved teacher practice, while others were categorized as unreasonable; for example, in all four schools, lesson plans as requested from the SEC had changed constantly, which proved a challenge for some departments. One subject coordinator in Saeed's school said, "Constant changes in lesson plans have increased our stress and affected our work negatively. The lesson plans are always changing. These changes are affecting the students and parents as well." However, Ahmed, another coordinator, viewed things differently:

> I don't have this problem (changes in lesson plans); I used to have it at the beginning of the reform. Maybe a new teacher will complain about it. Now most of my teachers have at least six years' experience working under the reform, because they have already gone through the process. (Ahmed, personal communication, January 12, 2012)

He believed that changing lesson plans was not a problem for the experienced teachers. This discussion shows the internal variation in teachers' views on policy changes, which may be due to personality differences.

Ultimately, leaders are trying to provide conditions for change, such as time, resources, and support, that can help their team to cope with their challenges. At the same time, leaders require conditions such as a collaborative and committed team in order to manage change. Conditions for change vary depending on the stage of the reform implementation. In some cases, followers need leadership and support more than resources and time. Teachers should be more involved in decision-making at the school level to help in reform implementation. School leaders' capacities are likely to increase considerably through encouragement and training, allowing them to use multiple frames to respond to organizational problems.

Section 2: Leaders' challenges in implementing the reform and how they responded to these issues

My third and fourth research questions asked about the challenges school leaders face when implementing the ENE reform and its requirements, further inquiring about their respective responses to these challenges. In this section, I outline challenges faced by leaders and their roles in managing them in order to address these two questions.

Theme 5: Overall perceptions of challenges

All the leaders across the four schools faced different challenges in leading the change. Some of these challenges were school-based internal issues such as interruptions and resistance to change. Also present were external pressures such as parental involvement and dealing with the SEC. These four challenges are all related to working with people both within and outside schools. The experiences described by the school leaders in this study reflect the socially driven transformational organizations described by Leithwood et al. (1999) and Muijs (2006), who report that the most problematic challenges for head teachers relate to dealing with the people within their organizations.

The schools also have challenges such as workload and student behavior, which were discussed in detail in the cases. Some of the causes of these challenges, such as lack of organization, heavy workload and lack of communication between the school and the SEC, are similar across the four schools. However, some of these reasons are institution-specific: for example, lack of organization is evident in Amna's school, while PD and teacher training are greater difficulties in Salwa's school. Covering lessons is more of a problem in the third school and student behavior more so in the fourth school. In this section, I will present the challenges, the reasons behind them, and the way in which the leaders tried to manage them.

Table 4 identifies dealing with the SEC to be the most prominent challenge faced by the four leaders. It is also apparent that Kawla's school faced all four challenges, for two reasons. Firstly, inexperienced teachers have difficulties in teaching the new curriculum. Most subject coordinators confirmed that the level of the subject is too high for the students and the curriculum is difficult for students at the primary level, with a resulting impact on students, teachers, and parents. Secondly, the school has problems with covering lessons because teachers refuse to take extra lessons, presenting leaders with another challenge.

Principals' challenges		Amna: Alnoor School	Salwa: Doha School	Kawla: Aljazeera School	Saeed: Gulf School
Internal	Interruptions	X	X	X	
	Resistance to change		X	X	X
External	Liaising with the SEC	X	X	X	X
	Parents	X		X	

Table 4. Leaders' challenges: the boxes crossed in the table show the existing problem faced by each leader (each challenge has been discussed in this section)

The findings of this study do not reflect the ways in which leaders learn from such situations. The school leaders agree that their experience and skills have improved, but they cannot articulate what has enabled them to learn. Research shows that as schools face continual challenges, key skills required of principals include not only the ability to deal with these challenges but also the ability to learn from them (Fullan & Miles, 1992). If leaders can learn from challenging situations and understand how they have learned, then they can adapt and deal with future problems.

Internal challenges

a) Interruptions

During my site visits, leaders and other teachers seemed to be always running: from a class, to a meeting, to a workshop, there was always something going on. Alnoor School principal Amna was constantly interrupted. For example, during my interview with her, she received two phone calls, and three teachers came to talk with her. She commented: "I have to be in three places at once in this school. I have to deal with students, buses, parents... everything." In general, she places great importance on being able to see people when they need to see her. During the interview she commented: "I operate an open-door policy for staff to talk to me about any issues or concerns." The Qatar school principal, Salwa, was also doing more than one task at the same time, some of which could have been undertaken by other members of staff. Whilst I was in Salwa's office, she was interrupted by four teachers within the space of 10 minutes, yet she managed to assuage their concerns in short order and also to complete her own tasks. Similarly, Ajazeera School principal Kawla was also doing several tasks at the same time. However, in the fourth school, the boys' school, I did not see any evidence of interruptions. This school was more organized, and the workload was reduced compared to the other schools. Leaders in these schools needed to be able to deal with unexpected tasks, while maintaining the flexibility to continue with their plan and their priorities among their regular daily tasks. Principals needed to delegate responsibilities or place limits with teachers, but some teachers were demonstrating indisputably codependent behaviors.

There are some reasons evident behind these interruptions. The school leaders are often so focused on dealing with parents and constant requests from the SEC, while putting in place basic procedures and trying to run the school more smoothly on the new system, that they sometimes do not pay adequate attention to core aspects of school administration. For example, I noticed that Alnoor School still does not have a clear procedure for student trips.

Another example I observed was one school's lack of basic procedures for effectively chairing and managing meetings. There was no minute-taking, and during the next meeting, the team spent time going over the main points of the previous meeting. During our interview with Amna, the principal, she seemed confident that the correct procedures were in place and responded to my question about parents' concern regarding their daughters' school trip safety, saying, "We have a clear procedure for trips." It emerged that the school held meetings to create policies and had spent time on this issue, having all the necessary paperwork and forms. However, this document-supported procedure was inexplicably not being followed.

Managing interruptions was always a challenge for leaders. Principals seemed not to know how to protect their time. Although aware of some of the reasons behind interruptions, such as the workload, the number of extracurricular activities, and high teacher turnover, principals had not recognized the other causes of problems, such as PD needs and the number of interruptions. For example, Kawla was constantly busy with minor issues and interruptions such as staff coming to ask about coloured ink for printers, organizing student trips, and student forms and thus failed to focus on her main tasks. This pattern occurred not only with Kawla but also with other leaders. Their job descriptions do not specify who should be doing what. As a result, she took some of her work home to finish or had to look for a quiet place to concentrate. Leaders therefore assumed too much work, while others relied on them for every small matter—an entirely unsustainable situation.

Most of the leaders were dealing with multiple tasks, one after another, and were so busy answering questions that they could not finish their work. However, I observed that some subject coordinators attempted to manage these interruptions. Reham, the English coordinator in the third school, said, "I have lots of interruptions, and I have my main task that I need to accomplish. I have to prioritize and do the urgent tasks, then the important tasks. For example, I was preparing my lessons for next week, but I had one teacher who was absent. It was essential to cover the lesson and not leave the class without a teacher." The capacity to manage a constantly changing workload is clearly essential to effective school leadership.

b) Resistance to change

Change may threaten and disturb organizations, but resistance to change can be constructive in identifying things that are going wrong (Fullan, 2001a). Ellsworth (2000) agrees with Fullan that resistance is a source of constructive diagnosis for change. However, the findings from this study show that resistance to change is a permanent difficulty in implementing the reform. Helping schools to overcome this resistance should be seriously considered. Rogers (1995) differentiates five categories of adopters by their willingness to accept an innovation: innovators, early adopters, early majority, late majority, and laggards. Accordingly, this study's findings show most of the teachers to fall in the last two categories. Those who join the reform late are more cautious and doubtful, not reacting until most others have done so. Laggards are the last to adopt innovation; they are very suspicious of change and reluctantly hang on to established values and traditions.

The findings from this study agree with the two forms of resistance suggested by Plant (1987), who states that resistance to change comes in two forms: systematic and behavioral. Systematic resistance occurs when there is a lack of knowledge, information, skills and managerial capacity, while behavioral resistance is more emotionally centered and derives from the reactions and perceptions of individuals and groups in the organization.

Salwa faced behavioral resistance from her teachers. Resisters are also a challenge for some of Salwa's subject coordinators. One remarked,

> In response to the reform we had three groups. There was a group of staff who were self-motivated risk takers who wanted to try new experiences. They accepted the change and joined the new system, because they had been fed up with the MoE. The second group were those who resisted the change at the beginning and that was not because they refused the change in itself, but because they didn't want

to change what they used to do. Behavioral resisters were those who resisted and didn't accept the change so couldn't continue in the independent schools. (Doha School teacher, personal communication, December 4, 2011)

The form of resistance in Amna's school fell in the third group who resisted the change and did not continue in the independent schools, leaning towards behavioral rather than systematic resistance. It is emotionally centered and teachers who are unable to cope with the change leave the school, causing the related problem of teacher turnover. Salwa regarded such leavers thus: "This group don't want to leave their comfort zone. They don't want to change what they are used to doing, what they are comfortable with." A clear example of systematic resistance is apparent in the coordinator's comment that "resisters don't accept the change, because they don't have enough information or skills to implement it." Thus, teachers can resist change, doing so both systematically and behaviorally.

Saeed classified teachers under the reform into three groups. The first group he called "normal/unremarkable teachers," a term he used to denote "the group that was satisfied with their ways of teaching. They like the MoE system, and their lesson plans had not changed for more than 10 years. They copy and paste without changes—they are not innovators." The second group he called "resisters to change," defining this group as "those who refused change most of the time and resisted. Sometimes they affect others negatively." The third group contained those "who don't know their position, one day they accept change and another day they resist."

As discussed in the literature review chapter, resistance has varied causes. The findings from this study agree with Connor's (1998) explanation that teachers resist change because of the uncertainty of its objectives, such as involvement in external programs and extracurricular activities. In addition, teachers need information about the benefits of the change and its method of introduction such as using the new assessment policy. Perceived threats to status also play a part, and teachers need new skills such as teaching advanced skills in math and science to cope with the change. If there is no training and support, then the change will be resisted.

Finally, power struggles constitute resistance to change. Samia and Raesa both face resistance from their staff because of a power struggle within each department. They were both clear about how staff perceived them to be too young and inexperienced to be heads of department. These two new leaders consequently faced staff collaboration challenges. Contrary to the findings reported by Daresh and Male (2000), the head teachers in early headship report no "settling in" period, emphasizing instead the expectation that they should go in, deal with challenges, and make strategic decisions from day one. There are significant implications here for the way in which new leaders are prepared for their leadership role, which are discussed later in the final chapter under the recommendations section.

Managing resistance to change and dealing with issues that relate to people and inter-staff relationships constitute real challenges for the leaders in this study. Similarly, Webb and Vulliamy (1996) identify working with and through people in organizations to be the dominant challenge for school leaders, who must simultaneously respond to rigid system expectations and accountability measures from the SEC. How to narrow down the cause(s) of resistance; how to avoid the pain, stress, and ambiguity of change; and how to manage resistance better are important aspects of leadership roles in any school setting, especially a Qatari school post-reforms.

Leaders were observed to use a number of strategies when trying to deal with resistance. These included listening to their team, trying to show them the benefit of the change, and choosing a positive coordinator to help manage the difficulties. Leaders confirmed that it was their responsibility to understand resistance to change and to try to manage it by identifying the causes. Saeed said, "I have to listen to the resisters, because as a leader I have to understand the reasons behind the resistance, and then provide solutions." Another coordinator tried to deal with resistant teachers by showing them the benefit of new methods. He confirmed that most of the time they "fall into line with the rest of the team."

Kawla reported that "we have teachers whose hobby is to say 'no' and resist everything. So, it is important to choose the coordinator, because if the coordinator is a positive person, then she can encourage her team. And we have really positive coordinators. We choose them very carefully." As Fullan (1993) and Sparks (1993) both point out, school leaders need to understand the change process in order to lead and manage change and improvement efforts effectively, so the school leader must learn to overcome barriers that exist during the complex process of change (Fullan & Miles, 1992).

However, Omar, Saeed's assistant, believed that they did not have resisters in his school; instead, he called them "less motivated staff." He said:

> We don't have teachers who resist change, because everyone knows that they don't have options—they have to follow these rules. I try to build teams that can support each other. I always make sure to have a combination of motivated and less motivated teachers, because they encourage each other. But I have to be careful about the less motivated staff; they can have a negative effect. (Omar, personal communication, January 10, 2012).

Leaders' own perceptions of reform-related challenges considerably influenced their ability to respond positively or negatively to the goal. To conclude, the difficulty of organizational change is often exacerbated by the mismanagement of resistance. Waddell and Sohal (1998) suggest that management may greatly benefit from techniques that carefully manage resistance to change by looking for ways of utilizing it, rather than overcoming it.

External challenges

a) Liaising with the SEC

Table 4 shows that liaising with the SEC is the most significant challenge in all the four schools. As mentioned earlier, most problems related to working with the SEC in previous sections are connected to constant change and workload. It is important to mention them here again, to demonstrate the overlap and the relationship between the themes, which, being interconnected, are difficult to present in isolation. Amna expressed disappointment when mentioning the SEC's lack of support, saying: "The reform is a good initiative, but the people who are running it are making our lives difficult." Her assistant agreed with her:

> Dealing with the SEC is stressful. Some parents are not happy about the new reform, though some of them are satisfied with it. But the problem is once again the SEC and how they treat us. Whether the parents are right or wrong, the SEC always sees them as being right. (Amna's assistant, personal communication, November 2, 2011)

Most subject coordinators did not have enough time to monitor their teachers and observe classrooms, because they had to finish the ongoing requests from the SEC. Leaders' efforts were redirected to paperwork and filing from classroom and student learning. As mentioned earlier in the "workload" theme, the ongoing requests from the SEC validated leaders' increasing workload. Teachers reported excessive amounts of paperwork, indicating that the time they spend preparing these folders could be used instead to focus more on learners and classrooms. However, some teachers complained that they had to follow orders. Samia repeated these words in her interview many times: "We have to do this and we should follow that, so we don't have any other choice. We have to convince our team, because it comes from the SEC." Similarly, Maryam said, "We don't have any other choice, we have to do this and we have to follow instructions," a situation also confirmed by Seham: "Even if we disagree with a new policy, we have to follow it because it's from the SEC." Another challenge from the SEC was what Salwa described as "urgent requests." She explained: "Sometimes the SEC requests something and asks us to send it the same day or the following day." Schools do not have a choice whether or not to respond, so their planning is constantly changing. However, some teachers believe that introducing new policies will be for the benefit of students. This is the case with Reshma, who maintains: "These orders were coming from the experts [in the SEC], so let's try it. What's the harm in trying new things? We'll know the advantages and disadvantages when we try it." As with other themes, I found different perceptions between leaders and their teachers about receiving new policies from the SEC.

The main aim of the reform is to give school leaders more autonomy, but under the current situation they are only implementers—a role similar to the one they had under the MoE. Interestingly, what the interviews do not reveal is any differentiation between the new and the more established leaders in dealing with the SEC. Almost all leaders admit to feeling pressured.

b) Communicating with parents

Parent involvement in schools has been the subject of many books and articles over the last 40 years. Fullan (2007) argues that educational reform confuses teachers, administrators and parents as well. Fullan (2007) states that "the closer the parent is to the education of the child, the greater the impact on child development and educational achievement" (2007, p. 189). But what type of involvement do Qatari schools need at this stage of the reform? Leaders in this study reported problems in working and communicating with parents. Amna complained about lack of policies and procedures for handling parental complaints, saying: "The SEC should think about why parents disagree with the new system, and consider what the real reasons behind their disagreement might be. Instead, the SEC is focusing on short-term ways to make the parents happy, doing whatever they can do for them, even sometimes asking us to apologize without giving us a chance to explain our actions." Her assistant, Reem, was more likely to consider that parents put additional demands on them, particularly in relation to teaching materials. She said: "Sometimes teachers make mistakes in spelling or on worksheets or other tiny mistakes. Parents then come and complain, and I think parents sometimes aren't aware of how they waste our time and effort. The problem is that the SEC has given them the right to do so." Fullan (2007) argues that decisions about the nature of parent involvement must take into account cultural, ethnic and class differences as well as variations related to the age and gender of students.

In Kawla's school, I had the chance to see a parent-teacher meeting. Most of the mothers at the meeting were pleased with the school. Recalling the mother who lauded the Aljazeera School—"There are great teachers who worked hard in this school…my daughter is happy now and so am I"—most teachers were positive with the mothers and gave feedback in a professional way. The Arabic coordinator (new in her position) expressed frustration that she did not know how to work constructively with some parents: "Some parents are supportive but most of them are not. The new system has given them the right to be decision-makers more than is necessary."

An example of positive interaction is the mothers' visits to the classroom as a part of the school's various ways of communicating with parents, so that parents could see the school in action. Nuzhat, a Grade 5 science teacher, was confident, although slightly nervous. Her head of department was available and supportive, saying, "You can do it, I'm sure you will be fine." After her lesson, she came to the teachers' room very pleased and proud of herself.

Saeed believed that he had solved the problem of dealing with parents, agreeing with the vice-principal that they had established the best way to communicate in this context. They both identified their relationships with parents as good, with Saeed commenting:

> Before, we had problems with parents, but now we have less misunderstanding. We gave parents the staff's mobile numbers, so they can communicate with teachers and coordinators directly. We also communicate with parents in different ways such as in parents' meetings and newsletters. In addition to these points of contact, parents can observe

classes and attend office hours. (Saeed, personal communication, January 9, 2012)

I asked Fahad about the communication between parents and staff. He said:

> I think this solution (giving parents the staff's mobile numbers) has more advantages than disadvantages. It is better that more communication between the school and parents can happen, because not all parents can come to the school—most of them are busy. The one significant disadvantage is that parents can call teachers during the weekend or at evening time, and this will annoy teachers. (Fahad, personal communication, January 8, 2012)

However, their teachers disagreed with leader-initiated solutions. There are communication problems and parental complaints to the SEC because schools do not solve problems in the way that parents would prefer. Schools also need support from parents in areas relating to homework, student learning and behavior.

To conclude, school leaders are working within a very stressful environment, but at the same time they also have opportunities to work better with parents and the wider community. Accordingly, Dolan (1994) argues:

> In a school, where mistrust between the community and the administration is the major issue, you must begin to deal with it by making sure that parents are at every major event, every meeting, every challenge. Within the discomfort of that presence the learning and healing could begin. (p. 60)

However, schools also need support from parents. In this regard, Hargreaves and Fullan (1998, pp. 124–125) suggest guidelines for parent actions, including:

- Press governments to create the kinds of teachers you want.
- Leave nostalgia behind you.
- Ask what you can do for your school, as well as what your school can do for you.
- Put praise before blame.

Parental interaction and communication management thus contribute to school leaders' challenges, which must be overcome to maintain focus on larger implementation strategies. Without an awareness of the need to manage interruptions, ongoing and important priorities are likely to suffer.

The four leaders face internal and external challenges. The school leaders were focusing on trying to manage the internal ones, for instance understanding the reasons behind any resistance and trying to support the resisters. However, they faced difficulties in dealing with the external challenges, such as those posed by the SEC. Although positivity towards the change could minimize the side effects of these challenges, the schools needed more support in sustaining the reform and managing their tasks under it. Lesson substitution and the curriculum content were examples of internal challenges for leaders in leading and managing the change. The SEC and parents were example sources of external difficulties. Finally, the leaders' way of dealing with the reform was also a factor in reducing the possibility of more challenges. Involving leaders in the decision-making, for example, and allowing for the organization of their time without interruptions can create a more supportive working environment.

Chapter Nine

LOOKING FORWARD: LESSONS LEARNED FROM THE QATARI EDUCATIONAL REFORM

This study set out to explore the perceptions of school leaders in four schools working within the context of the ENE reform in Qatar. The study also sought to explore the challenges that these leaders are facing in managing the school community. Reiterating my thoughts that this book does not take the one-size-fits-all approach to propose quick-fix solutions or ready-made answers. Hence, in this chapter, I summarize the main findings of this research, that leads to the lessons learned from the Qatari educational reform.

There is a clear research gap on the roles of Qatari school leaders, their experiences, and their problems in managing the educational reform. Leadership research identifies school leaders as the key ingredient in successful schools, and this study has presented empirical data to present and dissect perceptions of school leaders implementing the reform in Qatar. Although the scope of the field work was limited to four schools, the study provides insight into the ways in which leaders delivering the reform may inform the educational research agenda in Qatar, particularly in relation to challenges encountered.

In addition, this study contributes to the literature on school leadership and school improvement through its emphasis on the principals' roles in managing the reform and their roles as change agents. Principals' roles are central to this study, and leadership literature highlights their critical contribution in improving teacher performance. Significantly, this study adds to the understanding of the nature of change as being a nonlinear, continuous process.

The main purpose of educational change, according to Atkin (2000), is to make an impact on the relevant practitioners' beliefs, skills and perspectives. However, there is variation between individual participants' understanding of the nature of that change or innovation. In the initial phase of change, the innovation's benefits must be clear to all participants (Fullan, 1991). In other words, individuals and institutions ought to know where they are heading (Hargreaves, 1997). Participant perceptions of the educational reform have been analysed and discussed in the findings chapter, with this study's main findings presented within the portrait and cross-case chapters, respectively (Chapters Five through Nine). The present section will synthesize these findings to answer the four research questions, the first two questions being:

1. How do school leaders interpret school change and its place in *Education for a New Era*?
and
2. What are leaders' roles in managing the reform?

In answer to these two questions, four themes emerged: workload, teamwork, emotional response to change and conditions for change. Firstly, with regard to workload, all principals admitted that the reform increased role- and task-based workload, which created a professional overload both during and after the working school day. This same theme, that of increased workload, was also highlighted in another Qatar-based study by Zellman et al. (2011). In evaluating the experience of Qatari teachers under the ENE reform, the authors of that study identified widespread teacher concern over demands for curriculum material development as a major deterrent to employment in independent Qatari schools.

The amount of work is similar in both male and female schools, but workload-related problems are worse in the latter. Leaders not only suffer under an immense workload, but also create it. In addition, the findings corroborate the belief held by most leaders that they possess inadequate time to manage the workload emerging from the ENE reform. Furthermore, my findings illustrate a lack of clear guidance from the SEC on implementing the reform requirements such as new assessment policy, curriculum content, lesson plan, and extracurricular activities. Workload perceptions varied between school leaders and some of their staff. Leaders viewing the new workload as manageable are typically those who organize their tasks, attempt to clarify new policies for themselves and their teachers, and see extra work as necessary for successful reform implementation. Effective school leadership, interdepartmental collaboration, and clarity in SEC policies will all significantly contribute to reducing this workload's negative impact.

Despite school leaders' generally positive view of the reform, they experienced the imposition of constantly changing SEC policies as detrimental to their work. School leaders face frequent policy changes, causing duplication of work, demanding a shift of teacher focus from classroom to administrative tasks, and most importantly obscuring the meaning of the 'change' concept. Fullan (1999) supports this view, arguing that clarity and complexity are often major problems in any reform. Leaders in this study faced ambiguity in implementing the reform's requirements: the system failed the leaders by not providing enough support; rather, it was the expectation that principals create their own path to implementation. Huberman and Miles (1984) found that abstract goals resulted in confusion, frustration, anxiety and abandoning of effort. To further support this view, Hall and Hord (2006) found that when leaders are facing innovation and change and lack understanding, actual implementation might well be inconsistent with the original plan.

In addition, though the reform was introduced nine years ago, new policies are still being created, resulting in a substantially increased workload. Prior to undertaking this study, as an insider who had experience (during 2005–2007) within the earlier ENE phases, I did not predict the subsequent and constant demands and changes from the SEC. Rather, I assumed that, a few years down the line, the reform policies would have stabilized, giving leaders and teachers a more manageable workload. This assumption was at odds with the ground reality I encountered during my fieldwork in 2011–12, in which case study participants were subject to continuous change and frequently contradictory instructions from the SEC, consequently resulting in a highly unpredictable and often deeply stressful workload. My assumption was also based on the schools' cohort one status. I had previously worked as a cohort two school leader, while I supposed that my cohort one colleagues would have benefited from being nine years into the change process in terms of workload familiarity. This prediction, too, proved highly inaccurate.

Based on this study's findings, there are several lessons to be learned in terms of workload. School leaders require strategies to reduce workload, specifically:

- reducing the amount of time spent on schoolwork at home or outside school hours;
- using support staff to relieve teachers of administrative duties such as photocopying;
- minimizing the number of meetings and using meeting time effectively;
- prioritizing tasks and filtering demands from external activities and programs;
- ensuring clarity of new policies, and effective communication at all levels, especially between the SEC and schools and between heads of department and teachers;
- communicating to the SEC about superfluous demands that interfere with education activities; and
- professional development training in time management.

In all four schools, the senior management work well together. However, each school struggles with instances of departmental non-collaboration. Collegial relationships among and between staff are an important feature of schools that are more successfully implementing the reform. According to Fullan and Hargreaves (1991), "in collaborative cultures, teachers develop the collective confidence to respond to changes critically, selecting and adapting those elements that will aid improvement in their own work context, and rejecting those that will not" (1991, p. 49). Another significant takeaway from this study is that each school needs to encourage a collaborative culture with the following features:

- regular opportunities for continuous improvement (Rosenholtz, 1989);
- teachers who are more likely to trust, value, and legitimize sharing expertise, seek advice, and help other teachers (Fullan & Hargreaves, 1991);
- more team teaching and shared decision-making (Fullan & Hargreaves, 1991);
- sharing resources and supplies, planning cooperatively, and developing a "common sense of accomplishment" and a strong sense of efficacy (Ashton & Webb, 1986, in Fullan & Hargreaves, 1991);
- teachers who regularly seek ideas from seminars, colleagues, conferences, and in-service workshops (Rosenholtz, 1989);
- increased external professional networking with other teachers, schools, programs, and restructuring associations; and
- a place where "continuous self-renewal is defined, communicated, and experienced as a taken-for-granted fact of everyday life [in the school]" (Rosenholtz, 1989, p. 74).

Emotional response to change can be positive or negative. Effective leaders play an important role in change management by using emotional intelligence and emotional resilience to cope with change-related difficulties. The participants in this study need clarity on how to deal with change clarification. The teachers already have a compelling reason to make the reform a success; however, they are struggling due to lack of clarity as to how to cope with the change. This confusion affects other areas of their professional and personal lives, resulting in increased stress, decreased focus, and a diminished sense of the value of the change. Leaders have solutions in place to deal with change inside their school. However, the policy change that comes from the SEC has not been clarified in terms of processes and procedures. These factors make everyone's job harder and their acceptance of change incredibly difficult.

The next two research questions are as follows:

3. What challenges do school leaders face at each level, organizational and individual, when implementing the *Education for a New Era* reform and its requirements?
and
4. How do school leaders respond to the challenges of implementing school change in policy practice?

All four schools were observed as experiencing internal and external challenges while implementing the reform. Challenges took the form of teacher resistance, lack of collaboration among staff and curriculum content delivery, all constituting internal challenges. External challenges include school-SEC and school-parent communication, which mainly occurred due to the SEC's constantly changing policies and a lack of staff training in managing the reform in all its complexity. While a positive attitude towards the change may minimize negative consequences of the challenge, each school demonstrates a need for targeted support in managing and sustaining its tasks under the reform. Involving leaders in decision-making, offering time management training, giving strategies for preventing interruptions—all of these are examples of the kind of support required in this context.

It is important to note the difference between the centralized requirements of the SEC and the requirements of each school placed on its own teachers and students. Currently, each of the four schools' particular interpretations of the reform requirements created and increased artificial workload, especially in girls' schools as compared to that of the boys' school. Differences also occurred between the responses to change in schools for students of different genders. Girls' schools' participants were anxious about the professional development (PD) program, being mindful of its potential negative impact on their own professional evaluations. The development program required them to attend for a specific number of hours and stay back after school time. In the boys' school, however, professional development was thought of as a support, and the school seemed flexible about hours spent on it.

It is noteworthy that despite the implementation challenges, all the participants had positive views about the reform. Leaders worked collaboratively and teachers experienced trust from their leaders. On the student level, teachers acknowleged students' ability to problem-solve in contrast to the traditional rote memorization skills since reform implementation. A key characteristic of all school leaders in this study is the determination to try to resolve the challenging situation. Their problems did not relate to the reform as a whole but to certain elements of the reform. They were concerned about the negative aspects of the reform for the learners and the teachers.

In all four schools, heads of department played important roles in providing their teachers with support and encouragement to cope with the change. The more time and space individual departments provided for teachers to work and learn together, the more noticeable was its team culture of sharing. In all the four schools, leaders provided conditions for change, including constructive feedback and sharing best practices. At the same time, leaders themselves as adopters of the reform need conditions such as a collaborative and committed team in order for successful implementation to occur.

The four case studies, presented through portraiture, have demonstrated the crucial role that stories can play during reform and subsequent research by incorporating both formal and informal narratives from school leaders and their teams into their own school story. I have illustrated the contradictions in their perceptions in a single story. This underlines the inherent ambiguities of leadership approach, while portraiture highlights its complex nature. School leaders in this study are both adopters and change agents, and yet, as individuals they attempt to meet all expectations in both roles. They are trying to provide leadership in a context characterized by feelings of stress associated with their role.

My contribution provides an in-depth analysis of the complexities of change within Qatari schools after the reform and makes available a plurivocal account for other researchers and practitioners. The four case studies featured have also contributed empirically to the portrait literature. Finally, I have made a further literature contribution through applying narrative and change theories to my in-depth case study context.

REFERENCES

Anderson, M. K., Alnaimi, T. N. & Alhajri, S. H. (2010). National Student Research Fairs as Evidence for Progress in Qatar's Education for a New Era. *Improving Schools*, 13, 235–248.

Beatty, B. (2002). Emotional Epistemologies and Educational Leadership: A Conceptual Framework. A paper presented at the American Educational Research Association, New Orleans. ED 468293.

Blase, J. & Blase, J. (2002). *Breaking the silence: Overcoming the problem of principal mistreatment of teachers*. Thousand Oaks: Sage.

Bolman, L. G. & Deal, T. E. (1991). What makes a team work? *Organizational-Dynamics*, 21(2), 34–44.

Bolman, L. G. & Deal, T. E. (2003). *Reframing organizations: artistry, choice, and leadership* (3rd ed.). San Francisco: Jossey-Bass.

Bottery, M. (2004). *The Challenges of Educational Leadership*. London: Paul Chapman.

Brewer, D., Augustine, C., Zellman, G., Goldman, C. H., Stasz, C. & Constant, L. (2007). *Education for a New Era: Design and Implementation of K–12 Education Reform in Qatar*, RAND Corporation (MG–548–QATAR).

Chirichello, M. (2002). Collective leadership: Sharing the principalship. *Principal*, 81(1), 46–51.

Cohen, L., Manion, L. & Morrison, K. (2007). *Research Methods in Education*. London: Routledge Falmer.

Coker, M. (2010). Qatar Rewrites ABCs of Mideast Education. Retrieved 17 January 17 2011, from The Wall Street Journal: http://online.wsj.com/article/SB10001424052748704247904575240083760987978.html?-mod=WSJ_World_MIDDLENews.

Connor, D. R. (1998). *Managing at the speed of change. How resilient managers succeed and prosper where others fail*. Chichester: Wiley.

Constant, L., Goldman, C. A., Zellman, G., Augustine, C. H., Galama, T., Gonzalez, G., et al. (2010). Promoting Quality and Variety through the Public Financing of Privately Operated Schools in Qatar. *Journal of School Choice*, 4(4), 450–473.

Crawford, M. (2007). Rationality and Emotion in Primary School Leadership: An Exploration of Key Themes. *Educational Review*, 59(1), 87–98.

Crawford, M. (2009). *Getting to the Heart of Leadership: Emotion and the Educational Leader*. London: Sage.

Daresh, J. & Male, T. (2000). Crossing the Border into School Leadership: Experiences of Newly Appointed British Headteachers and American Principals. *Educational Management and Administration*, 28(1), 89–101.

Davenport, R. & Anderson, G. (2002). *Closing the achievement gap: No excuse*. Houston, Texas: American Productivity & Quality Centre.

Davies, B. (2005). *The Essentials of School Leadership*. London: Paul Chapman.

Day, C., Harris, A., Hadfield, M., Tolley, H. & Beresford, J. (2000). *Leading schools in times of change*. Buckingham: Open University Press.

Day, C., Sammons, P., Hopkins, D., Harris, A., Leithwood, K., Gu, Q. & Brown, E. (2010). *10 Strong Claims about Successful School Leadership*. College for Leadership of Schools and Children's Services.

Dolan, P. (1994). *Restructuring Our Schools*. Kansas City, Mo.: Systems & Organizations.

Dooley, K. (1999). Towards a Holistic Model for the Diffusion of Educational Technologies: An Integrative Review of Educational Innovation Studies. *Educational Technology & Society*, 2(4).

Drucker, P. (1995). *Managing in a time of great change*. New York: Talley House, Dutton.

Duignan, P. (2006). *Educational Leadership: Key Challenges and Ethical Tensions*. New York: Cambridge University Press.

Ellsworth, J. B. (2000). Surviving Change: A survey of educational change models. Retrieved January 2011, from http://www.ericit.org/digests/EDO–IR–2000–07.html.

Ely, D. P. (1990). Conditions that facilitate the implementation of educational technology innovations. *Journal of Research on Computing in Education*, 23(2), 298–305.

Ely, D. P. (1999). New perspectives on the implementation of educational technology innovation. Paper delivered at the Association for Educational Communications and Technology Annual Conference, Houston, TX, Feb., 1999.

English, F. (2000). A Critical Appraisal of Sara Lawrence-Lightfoot's *Portraiture* as a Method of Educational Research. *Educational Researcher*, 29(7), 21–26.

Evans, R. (1996). *The human side of school change*. San Francisco, CA: Jossey-Bass.

Everard, B., Morris, G. & Wilson, I. (2004). *Effective school management* (4th ed.). London: Paul Chapman.

Flin, R. (1996). *Sitting in the Hot Seat. Leaders and Teams for Critical Incident Management*. Chichester: Wiley.

French, R. (2001). 'Negative capability': Managing the confusing uncertainties of change. *Journal of Organizational Change Management*, 14(5), 480–492.

Fullan, M. G. (1991). *The New Meaning of Educational Change*. London: Cassell.

Fullan, M. G. (1993). The complexity of the change process. In *Change Forces: Probing the Depths of Educational Reform* (pp. 19–41). London: Falmer Press.

Fullan, M. G. (1999). *Change Forces: The sequel.* Philadelphia, PA: Falmer Press.

Fullan, M. G. (2001a). *Leading in a culture of change.* San Francisco: Jossey-Bass.

Fullan, M. G. (2001b). *The New Meaning of Educational Change* (3rd ed.). New York: Teachers College Press.

Fullan, M. G. (2002). The Change Leader. *Educational Leadership.* EBSCO Publishing.

Fullan, M. G. (2006). The future of educational change: system thinkers in action. *Journal of Educational Change, 7,* 113–122.

Fullan, M. (2007). *The New Meaning of Educational Change* (4th ed.). New York: Teachers College Press.

Fullan, M. G. & Hargreaves, A. (1991). What's Worth Fighting for in Your School? Toronto: Ontario Public School Teachers' Federation; Andover, Mass.: The Network; Buckingham, UK: Open University Press; Melbourne: Australian Council of Educational Administration.

Fullan, M. G. & Miles, M. B. (1992). Getting the reform right: What works and what doesn't. *Phi Delta Kappan, 73*(10), 745–752.

Fullan, M. & Stiegelbauer, S. (1991). *The new meaning of educational change* (2nd ed.).New York: Teachers College Press.

Gonzalez, G., Karoly, L. A., Constant, L., Salem, H. & Goldman, C. A. (2008). *Facing Human Capital Challenges of the 21st Century, Education and Labor Market Initiatives in Lebanon, Oman, Qatar, and the United Arab Emirates.* USA: Rand-Qatar Policy Institute.

Groves, K., McEnrue, M. & Shen, W. (2008) Developing and measuring the emotional intelligence of leaders. *Journal of Management Development,* 27(2), 225–250.

Hackmann, G. D. G. (2002). Using portraiture in educational leadership research. *International Journal of Leadership in Education: Theory and Practice,* 5(1), 51–60.

Hall, G. E. & Hord, S. M. (1987). *Change in schools: Facilitating the process.* Albany, NY: State University of New York Press.

Hall, G. E. & Hord, S. M. (2006). *Implementing change: Patterns, principles, and potholes* (2nd ed.). Boston: Pearson/Allyn & Bacon.

Hargreaves, A. (1997). Rethinking Educational change: Going deeper and wider in the quest for success. In A. Hargreaves (Ed.), ASCD Yearbook, *Rethinking educational change with heart and mind (pp. 1–26).* Alexandria, Virginia: Association for Supervision and Curriculum Development.

Hargreaves, A. & Fullan, M. (1998). *What's Worth Fighting for Out There.* New York: Teachers' College Press.

Hord, S. M., Rutherford, W. L., Huling-Austin, L. & Hall, G. E. (1987). *Taking Charge of Change*. Alexandria, VA: Association of Supervision and Curriculum Development.

Horng, E., Kalogrides, D., & Loeb, S. (2010). Principal preferences and the unequal distribution of principals across schools (Working Paper No. 36). Washington, DC: Urban Institute, National Center for Analysis of Longitudinal Data in Education Research.

Hoy, W. K. & Tschannen-Moran, M. (1999). The five faces of trust: An empirical confirmation in urban elementary schools. *Journal of School Leadership*, 9, 184–208.

Huberman, M. & Miles, M. (1984). *Innovation up close*. New York: Plenum.

Huy, Q. N. (2002). Emotional balancing of organizational continuity and radical change: The contribution of middle managers. *Administrative Science Quarterly*, 47(1), 31–69.

James, C. & Connolly, U. (2000). *Effective change in schools*. London; New York: RoutledgeFalmer.

Jaworski, B. (2003). Researching practice into/influencing mathematics teaching and learning development: Towards a theoretical framework based on co-learning partnerships. *Educational Studies in Mathematics*, 54(1), 249–282.

Johnson, A. M. (1998). A response to restructuring: The dilemmas of school principals in a process of change. *The Urban Review*, 30(4), 309–332.

Johnson, S. M. (1990). The Primacy and Potential of High School Departments. In M.W. McLaughlin, J. E. Talbert & N. Bascia (Eds.). *The Contexts of Teaching in Secondary Schools: Teachers' Realities* (pp. 123–140). New York: Teachers College Press.

Keeton, K., Fenner, D. E., Johnson, T. R. B. & Hayward, R. A. (2007). Predictors of physician career satisfaction, work-life balance, and burnout. *Obstetrics & Gynecology*, 109(4), 949–955.

Knight, J. (2014). Understanding education hubs within the context of cross-border education. In J. Knight (Ed.), *International education hubs: student, talent, knowledge-innovation* (pp. 13–28). Dordrecht: Springer.

Kotter, J. (2002). *The Heart of Change: Real-Life Stories of How People Change Their Organizations*. Harvard: Harvard Business Press.

Kyriacou, C. (2001). Teacher Stress: Directions for future research. *Educational Review*, 53(1), 27–35.

Lawrence-Lightfoot, S. (1983). *The Good High School*. New York: Basic Books.

Lawrence-Lightfoot, S. & Hoffman Davis, J. (1997). *The Art and Science of Portraiture*. San Francisco: Jossey-Bass.

Leedy, P. D. & Ormrod, J. E. (2005). *Practical research: Planning and design* (8th ed.). Upper Saddle River, NJ: Prentice Hall.

Leithwood, K. A. & Jantzi, D. (1990). Transformational leadership: How principals can help reform school cultures. Paper presented at the Canadian Association for Curriculum Studies, Victoria, British Columbia, Canada.

Leonard, P. (1996). Variations in values orientations in the implementation of multi-grades: Implications for Moral Leadership. *Canadian Journal of Educational Administration and Policy*, 5, 11 January 1996.

Levine, D. K. & Lezotte, L. W. (1990). *Unusually Effective Schools: A Review and Analysis of Research and Practice*. Madison, Wise: National Centre for Effective School Research and Development.

Little, J. W. (2003). Inside teacher community: Representations of classroom practice. *Teachers College Record*, 105(6), 913–945.

Louis, K. S., Leithwood, K., Wahlstrom, K. L., & Anderson, S.E. (2010). Investigating the links to improved student learning: Final report of research findings. Retrieved from Wallace Foundation website: http://www.wallacefoundation.org/knowledge-center/school-leadership/key-research/Pages/Investigating-the-Links-to-Improved-StudentLearning.aspx

Marshall, J. M., Brooks, J. S., Brown, K. M., Bussey, L. H., Fusarelli, B., Gooden, M. A., et al. (Eds.) (2012). *Juggling flaming chain saws: Faculty in educational leadership try to balance work and family*. Charlotte, NC: Information Age Publishing.

McLaughlin, M. W. & Mitra, D. L. (2001). Theory-based change and change-based theory: Going deeper, going broader. *Journal of Educational Change*, 3(1), 301–323.

McLaughlin, M. W. & Talbert, J. E. (2001). *Professional communities and the work of high school teaching*. Chicago: University of Chicago Press.

Muijs, D. (2006). New Directions for School Effectiveness Research: Towards School Effectiveness without Schools. *Journal of Educational Change*, 7, 141–160.

Nasser, R. & Romanowski, M. H. (2011). Teacher Perceptions of Training in the Context of the Qatari National Educational Reform. *International Journal of Training and Development*, 15(2), 158–168.

Orr, M. T., Byrne-Jimenez, M., McFarlane, P. & Brown, B. (2005). Leading out from low performing schools: The urban principal experience. *Leadership and Policy in Schools*, 4(1), 23–54.

Paton, R. A. & McCalman, J. (2008). *Change Management: A Guide to Effective Implementation* (3rd ed.). London: Sage.

Peterson, K. D. & Brietzke, R. (1994). *Building collaborative cultures: Seeking ways to reshape urban schools*. In Urban Monograph Series. Oak Brook, IL: North Central Regional Educational Laboratory.

Peterson, K. D. & Deal, T. E. (2002). *Shaping school culture fieldbook*. San Francisco: Jossey-Bass.

Planning Council, Government of Qatar (2007). Labor Market Strategy for the State of Qatar: Main Report, Volume 1, 2nd version. Doha: Planning Council Publications.

Plant, R. (1987). *Managing change and making it stick*. London: Fontana.

Qatar Knowledge Economy Project (2007). Turning Qatar into a Competitive Knowledge-Based Economy.

Qatar Statistics Authority (2019). Qatar Statistical Authority: Population Structure.

Ravitz, J. (1999). Conditions that facilitate teachers' internet use in schools with high internet activity. Unpublished doctoral dissertation, Syracuse University, Syracuse, NY. (ERIC Document Reproduction Service ED 423855).

Rogers, E. M. (1995). *Diffusion of Innovations* (4th ed.). New York, NY: The Free Press.

Rosenholtz, S. (1989). *Teachers' Workplace*. New York: Longman.

Schlectly, P. (2002). *Working on the work*. San Francisco, CA: Jossey-Bass.

Scribner, J. P., Sawyer, R. K., Watson, S. T. & Myers, V. L. (2007). Teacher Teams and Distributed Leadership: A Study of Group Discourse and Collaboration. *Educational Administrative Quarterly*, 43(1), 67–100.

Sergiovanni, T. J. (1992). *Moral Leadership: Getting to the Heart of School Improvement*. San Francisco: Jossey-Bass.

Sherry, L., Billig, S., Tavalin, F., & Gibson, D. (2000). New insights on technology adoption in schools. *T.H.E. Journal*, 27, 43–46.

Shields, C. (2004). Dialogic leadership for social justice: Overcoming pathologies of silence. *Educational Administration Quarterly*, 40(1), 109–132.

Smollan, R. K., Sayers, J. G. & Matheny, J. A. (2010). Emotional responses to the speed, frequency and timing of organizational change. *Time and Society*, 19(1), 28–53.

Sparks, D. (1993). *Thirteen tips for managing change*. Wisconsin School News.

Thomson, P. (2002). *Schooling the rustbelt kids: making the difference in changing times*. Sterling USA, Stoke-on-Trent: Trentham Books Ltd.

Timperley, H. & Robinson, V. (2000). Workload and the Professional Culture of Teachers. *Educational Management & Administration*, 28(1), 47–62.

Travers, C. J. & Cooper, C. (1996). *Teachers under pressure: stress in the teaching profession*. London: Routledge.

US Library of Congress, Country Studies/Country Profile—Qatar, n.d. Available at: http://lcweb2.loc.gov/frd/cs/qatoc.html.

Waddell, D. & Sohal, A. S. (1998). Resistance: a constructive tool for change management. *Management Decision*, 36(8), 543–548.

Waterhouse, J. (2007). From narratives to portraits; methodology and methods to portray leadership. *The Curriculum Journal*, 18(3), 271–286.

Waterhouse, J. (2012). School Leadership in Context: Three Portraits. Cambridge Thesis submitted for PhD award.

Watts, J. H. (2009). 'Allowed into a man's world' meanings of work-life balance: Perspectives of women civil engineers as 'minority' workers in construction. *Gender, Work, and Organization,* 16(1), 37–57.

Webb, R. & Vulliamy, G. (1996). *Roles and Responsibilities in the Primary School: Changing Demands, Changing Practices*. Buckingham: Open University Press.

West-Burnham, J. (1997). *Managing Quality in Schools* (2nd ed.), Pearson Professional Limited.

Yukl, G. A. (2002). *Leadership in Organizations* (5th ed.). Upper Saddle River, NJ: Prentice Hall.

Zellman, G. L., Constant, L. & Goldman, C. A. (2011). *K–12 Education Reform in Qatar*. Santa Monica, CA: The RAND Corporation.

Zellman, G. L., Ryan, G. W., Karam, R., Constant, L., Salem, H., Gonzalez, G. C., et al. (2009). *Qatar's K–12 Education Reform Has Achieved Success in Its Early Years*. Santa Monica, CA: The RAND Corporation.